A COMPANION GUIDE
TO THE SCOTTISH NATIONAL
GALLERY OF MODERN ART

PATRICK ELLIOTT

A Companion Guide to the Scottish National Gallery of Modern Art

NATIONAL GALLERIES OF SCOTLAND
EDINBURGH · 1999

Published 1999 by the Trustees
of the National Galleries of Scotland

© The Trustees of the National Galleries of Scotland
ISBN 0 903598 84 1

Designed and typeset in FF Quadraat by Dalrymple
Printed in China by Toppan Printing Company
(Shenzhen Limited)

Frontispiece:
Joan Miró *Head of a Catalan Peasant (Tête de paysan Catalan)*, 1925
Purchased jointly with the Tate Gallery, London, with assistance
from the National Art Collections Fund 1999

Foreword

In recent years the National Galleries of Scotland have become increasingly active in organising major loan exhibitions, yet we have been equally active in expanding our permanent collections and making them better known. Besides making many outstanding additions to our collections we have also published concise, illustrated catalogues of the works belonging to the Scottish National Gallery of Modern Art, Scottish National Portrait Gallery and National Gallery of Scotland.

This fully-illustrated *Companion Guide* to the Gallery of Modern Art marks another step towards enhancing public awareness of our remarkable collections. A second volume on the Scottish National Portrait Gallery is also available, and a third volume on the National Gallery collection is in preparation. Lavishly illustrated, informative and reasonably priced, these books will, we trust, allow more and more people to share in the enjoyment of our collections, and encourage more and more to visit the National Galleries of Scotland.

TIMOTHY CLIFFORD
Director, National Galleries of Scotland

Introduction

This is the first comprehensive *Companion Guide* to the collection of the Scottish National Gallery of Modern Art. Even so, the selection reproduced here – some 230 works spanning a hundred year period – represents just a fraction of the Gallery's collection, which now stands at some 5,000 items. The Gallery opened in August 1960 at Inverleith House, a handsome building of the 1770s set in the middle of Edinburgh's Royal Botanic Garden. The Gallery of Modern Art is the younger partner in the triumvirate of galleries which make up the National Galleries of Scotland. The National Gallery of Scotland opened on The Mound in central Edinburgh in 1859, and houses art mainly from the early Renaissance to the Post-Impressionists. The Scottish National Portrait Gallery opened in Edinburgh in 1889 and is devoted to portraiture, chiefly though not exclusively of Scots. The three galleries, which are funded by government, share the same Director and Board of Trustees but have separate Keepers.

The collection of the Scottish National Gallery of Modern Art spans the period from about 1890 to the present day, beginning with Vuillard, Bonnard and Matisse, and British artists such as Sickert, Orpen and William Nicholson. The earliest painting in the collection is Vuillard's *The Chat* of c.1892 (see p.14) while the earliest graphic works are etchings by Max Klinger dating from the early 1880s. There is in fact some overlap between the collections of the National Gallery and the Gallery of Modern Art, with the National Gallery displaying a few early twentieth-century works of Victorian character and also major Post-Impressionist works of the 1890s by Gauguin and Cézanne, for example. Of the five thousand works in the Gallery of Modern Art's collection, approximately half are prints (etchings, lithographs, wood engravings etc.) and of the remaining 2,500 works, again about half are drawings. The rest are predominantly paintings and sculptures. Most of the works reproduced in this book are paintings and sculptures, but a few of the major drawings and prints are also included, alongside a small number of artists' books. The collection is specifically of western art, and is primarily of western European art. American art is represented almost exclusively by postwar work. A *Concise Catalogue* of the collection, listing every item and reproducing many of the paintings, sculptures and drawings, was published in December 1993.

Nearly all the works in the collection have been acquired since 1960. Prior to this the National Gallery of Scotland did not collect the work of living artists; indeed there was an unwritten policy that an artist had to have been dead for at least ten years to qualify for inclusion in the collection. (This 'rule' stemmed not from a dislike of modern art, but was conceived as a way of controlling the growth of the collection.) A handful of exceptions were made, most of them originating in gifts or bequests. Notable among these are Oskar Kokoschka's *Zrání* (see p.63) which was acquired during the Second World War as a gift from the Czechoslovak Government in Exile; Emile-Antoine Bourdelle's sculpture *The Virgin of Alsace* (see p.23) which was purchased in 1930, the year after the artist's death; a few paintings by the Scottish Colourists, including Peploe's *The Black Bottle* (see p.90) and Leslie Hunter's *Reflections Balloch* (see p.97), both of which were given to the Gallery a few years after the artists' deaths; and three collections of prints which were acquired *en bloc* in the 1940s and which included a substantial number of contemporary etchings and wood engravings. In all, thirty-eight paintings and sculptures and about 500 graphic works were transferred from the National Gallery of Scotland to the Scottish National Gallery of Modern Art when it opened in 1960.

Apart from the above-mentioned exceptions, the Gallery's permanent collection has been assembled since 1960, either by purchase, gift or bequest. The National Gallery of Scotland owned important late nineteenth-century paintings by artists such as Van Gogh and Gauguin, and it was intended that the new Gallery of Modern Art should acquire international works of similar stature, and not simply represent Scottish art. The first acquisitions were a portrait by Sickert, bought in 1959 before the Gallery had even opened its doors, a figure painting by Matthew Smith, and Henry Moore's large bronze sculpture, *Two-Piece Reclining Figure* of 1960. To mark the opening of the Gallery, Alexander (later Sir Alexander) Maitland QC, a Trustee, donated an important group of paintings in memory of his wife, Rosalind. These included a 'Blue period' painting by Picasso (see p.18), two Vuillards, and a Rouault (see pp.14 and 19), though they were initially hung at the National Gallery as part of Maitland's extraordinary gift of French late nineteenth- and early twentieth-century paintings. On Maitland's death in 1965 the Rouault and Picasso were transferred to the Gallery of Modern Art, together with Matisse's *Painting Lesson* of 1919 (see p.26), which Maitland left to the Gallery in his will. The Vuillards, two Bonnards and Maillol's bronze sculpture *Eve with the Apple* (see p.22) were transferred to the Gallery of Modern Art in 1984.

At first, the Director of the National Galleries of Scotland, David Baxandall, ran the new Gallery with his Assistant Keeper (later Director) Colin Thompson, but in 1961 a Keeper of the Gallery of Modern Art was appointed, Douglas Hall. Hall remained Keeper until his retirement in 1986, and the quality and depth of

Inverleith House, Royal Botanic Garden, Edinburgh, home of the Scottish National Gallery of Modern Art from 1960 to 1984.

the collection are due in part to his pioneering efforts. The initial purchase grant accorded by the Treasury to the Gallery of Modern Art was £7,500, a sum Baxandall considered hopelessly inadequate for the job of 'illustrating the more important moments in the development of modern painting ... from fauves and cubists onwards'. Given these limited resources, the collection could never aspire to represent every major artist, nor could it offer a complete history of the development of modern art. But rather than fall to the temptation quickly to fill the Gallery with less expensive works, Hall chose to buy selectively and plug the gaps with loans from private collections. In its first year, the Gallery received several impressive gifts, including a painting by Edward Wadsworth presented by Mr and Mrs J. H. MacDonell in 1960 (see p.118), and a painting by William Roberts (see p.105) and a sculpture by Zadkine, both given by Miss Elizabeth Watt in 1961. Miss Watt later bequeathed her entire collection to the Gallery.

Many of the early purchases were of British, and particularly Scottish art, and foreign art was represented primarily through prints and works placed on loan. Among the early purchases were paintings by Paul Nash (*Landscape of the Vernal Equinox*, see p.127), Ivon Hitchens, Graham Sutherland (*Western Hills*, see p.126), John Maxwell's *View from a Tent* (see p.117), and a watercolour by David Jones. The first major foreign purchases were Larionov's *Soldier in a Wood* and Goncharova's *Rabbi with Cat* (see pp.50–51), which were included in a touring exhibition arranged by the Arts Council; at just £225 each they were discerning buys in 1962. The funds were provided by an anonymous donor from Edinburgh who gave £500 for the Gallery to spend as it wished.

Another shrewd early purchase was Kirchner's *Japanese Theatre* (see p.45), a masterpiece of German Expressionist painting dating from c.1909, which was bought from the Marlborough Gallery in London in 1965 for just under £20,000. By this date the Gallery's annual purchase grant had been raised to £20,000, in recognition of its need to 'catch up'. This figure compared favourably with the combined purchase grant for the National Gallery and Portrait Gallery of £25,000. Two other important paintings by artists associated with German Expressionism, Jawlensky and Nolde (see pp.48–49), were acquired in the 1960s. Works by the giants of modern art, such as Picasso, Matisse and Brancusi, were exceedingly expensive, even in the 1960s, but the Gallery was quick to buy the work of major postwar artists, including Dubuffet, Karel Appel and Nicolas de Staël (see pp.142 and 147). A drawing by Jackson Pollock was bought in 1963 (see p.145) but the Gallery's relationship to contemporary art, given its limitations of space and especially funding, was problematical: before 1972, Abstract Expressionism was represented only by works on paper. As Hall subsequently wrote, '... the responsibility of the Gallery was not wholly or even mainly to contemporary art. As an extension to the National Gallery of Scotland, which effectively stops its collection at Cézanne, it had already half a century of art to cover.' This inevitably meant that many of the radical developments of the 1960s which succeeded Abstract Expressionism were not collected by the Gallery .

It was only in 1966 that the first masterpiece of French modern art was bought, Léger's *Woman and Still Life* of 1921 (see p.33), for £15,000. Léger's dealer, Paul Rosenberg, had acquired the work from the artist in 1921, and it remained with the Rosenberg family until it was bought by the Gallery. The following year, 1967, the Gallery bought Picasso's still life *The Soles* 1940 (see p.132) at auction for £16,225. That same year a late painting by André Masson was also acquired, the first work by one of the Surrealists to enter the collection.

The Gallery's collection of Scottish art is broad and fairly representative, thanks largely to gifts and bequests. In 1967 Mr and Mrs Scott Hay gave a collection of mainly Scottish paintings by artists such as Joan Eardley and Robin Philipson, and ten years later Dr Robert Lillie bequeathed more than 300 works, again mainly by Scottish artists (the gift included 167 works by William Gillies: see p.116). Important donations made in recent years include over 250 drawings by Joan Eardley presented in 1987 by the artist's sister, Pat Black, and a fine group of works by John Maxwell and others bequeathed in 1988 by George and Isobel Neillands. In 1997 the distinguished painter Alan Davie, who had trained at Edinburgh College of Art before the war, gave the Gallery a large collection of his paintings, gouaches, brush drawings and prints from all periods of his career (see p.154–55).

By 1970 the annual purchase grant had risen to £72,000, and that year the Trustees took the decision to set aside £25,000 per annum 'for buying expensive works historically essential to the collection'. In this way it was possible, in 1973, to buy an important landscape painting by André Derain (see p.20) dating from the early stages of Fauvism. A bronze Cubist sculpture by Jacques Lipchitz was bought in 1968 (see p.31), but the Gallery's first Cubist painting, Braque's *The Candlestick* (see p.28), was not acquired until 1976. Major acquisitions of the late 1970s included Duane Hanson's *Tourists* (see p.194), bought at auction in New York in 1979, and Miró's *Painting* of 1925, again bought in 1979 and the first Miró to enter the collection (see p.70). Perhaps the finest acquisition of the early 1980s was Lichtenstein's *In the Car* (see p.168) bought in 1980, amid much controversy,

The Scottish National Gallery of Modern Art, Edinburgh (the former John Watson's School).

for £100,000. Richard Long's *Stone Line*, also bought in 1980, and César's *Compression*, bought in 1982, provoked similarly strong feelings (see pp.199 and 173). By 1985 the Gallery's share of the purchase grant had grown to £624,000, out of a total of nearly £1.5m for all three of the National Galleries. Thanks to this, it was possible to acquire important paintings by Delaunay, Léger and Balthus (see pp.35, 137–38).

The small size of Inverleith House meant that it was always seen as a temporary home for the Gallery of Modern Art. In 1984 the Gallery moved into much larger premises in the former John Watson's School, an imposing neo-classical building designed by William Burn in 1825 as an institution for fatherless children. Lying to the west of the city centre, the building offered approximately four times as much exhibition space as Inverleith House, and also provided room for more staff, conservation workshops (shared with the National Gallery and the Portrait Gallery), a print-room, café and shop. The extra space also meant that the Gallery could take or organize loan exhibitions on a regular basis, and the extensive grounds have proved an ideal location for the siting of large sculptures.

A couple of years after the move to the new building, Douglas Hall retired, making way for his successor. I had worked as Hall's research assistant from 1977–79 before leaving for the Tate Gallery in London. In 1987 I returned to Edinburgh to become the Gallery's second Keeper. In the late 1980s the prices for classic modern and even contemporary art rocketed to levels few could have forecast at the beginning of the decade. Yet despite the wildly increasing prices, and the fact that the larger part of the purchase grant has been centralised by Trustees (and the grant itself severely cut by government for much of the 1990s) some of the greatest works in the Gallery's collection have been bought over the last decade, including a number of 'firsts' (e.g. Charles Rennie Mackintosh and Lucian Freud, see pp.86–87 and 181) and some striking additions to the Gallery's holdings of German Expressionism and French painting (e.g. Vuillard and Barlach, see pp.15 and 61). This apparent paradox is due in part to the increasingly crucial role undertaken by private foundations and charities such as the National Art Collections Fund and the Henry Moore Foundation, and the publicly funded National Heritage Memorial Fund. Fiscal concessions – for example, private treaty sales, exempted works and 'in lieu' arrangements – have also made a significant contribution. A few of the more obvious remaining gaps have been filled with loans from private collections.

The most outstanding acquisitions of recent years have come from two sources, Sir Roland Penrose (1900–84) and Mrs Gabrielle Keiller (1908–95). Penrose owned what was probably the greatest private collection of twentieth-century art ever assembled in Britain. He acquired most of his works in the 1930s, when he established friendships with many of the French Surrealists and also with Picasso, whose biography he wrote. From time to time he would sell off individual works, and in 1982 the Gallery was offered Picasso's *Guitar, Gas-jet and Bottle*, a Cubist painting of 1912–13, which we purchased (see p.29). Following Penrose's death in 1984, his estate placed a number of works on loan, including an important early Henry Moore (*The Helmet*, see p.128) and Miró's *Maternity* (see p.71). In 1991 the Gallery was able to purchase the Miró painting, thanks to substantial grants from the National Heritage Memorial Fund and the National

Art Collections Fund. The Moore sculpture was purchased in 1992, with the assistance of the NHMF, NACF and Henry Moore Foundation. In 1994 we acquired (again with NHMF and NACF support) Penrose's library and archive, which included a large number of rare books by artists such as Kandinsky and Picasso (see pp.54 and 135).

When the National Lottery was launched in late 1994, the Gallery was an early beneficiary of one of its five 'good causes', the Heritage Lottery Fund. A grant of £3 million, awarded in 1995, allowed us to buy a collection of twenty-six paintings and drawings from the Penrose collection, including works by Dalí, Delvaux, Ernst, Man Ray, Magritte and Picasso. Later that year, the Gallery received easily the most important gift in its history, the collection of Gabrielle Keiller. Although she had never lived in Scotland, Mrs Keiller had, by chance, been born in East Lothian, where her parents were taking a golfing holiday. (She herself would become one of England's leading women golfers.) She subsequently married a Scot, the archaeologist Alexander Keiller, and after his death developed a close connection with the Gallery of Modern Art, becoming a much-valued advisor to our acquisitions committee from 1978 to 1985. She began collecting the work of Eduardo Paolozzi in the early 1960s and through him became interested in Dada and Surrealism, which she collected with passion and discrimination. We exhibited a large part of her collection during the 1988 Edinburgh Festival, when she decided to leave it to the Gallery in her Will. The following year she very generously gave us one of the original de-luxe versions of Marcel Duchamp's *Boîte-en-valise* (see p.66). In the early 1990s she sold a few works to the Gallery, including a Picabia of 1916–17 (see p.64), a rare wooden sculpture by Giacometti and a unique shaped canvas by Magritte (see pp.76 and 78), the last two previously owned by Roland Penrose. The substantial remainder of her collection she bequeathed on her death in December 1995. The complete collection includes some two hundred paintings, sculptures, drawings and prints, as well as a remarkable library of rare books, periodicals and manuscripts

The Dean Gallery extension to the Scottish National Gallery of Modern Art, opened in 1999.

related to the Surrealist movement. Highlights include Magritte's *The Magic Mirror* (see p.79) and works by Delvaux, Duchamp and Max Ernst; and a large body of work by Paolozzi. Three of the works, by Bacon, Ernst and Tanguy, were accepted by H. M. Government in lieu of inheritance tax on Mrs Keiller's estate and presented to the Gallery in 1998.

So it is that through a combination of deliberate policy and good fortune we have built up one of the world's great holdings of Dada and Surrealist art. Gaps in the rest of the collection of course remain. Although Gabrielle Keiller gave the Gallery its first Warhol – a popular portrait of her dog, Maurice (see p.169) – it may be difficult for us now to acquire a major Warhol of the 1960s. By the same token it is unlikely that we will ever be able to acquire a sculpture by Brancusi or a painting by Kandinsky. Having said this, when we published the *Concise Catalogue* of the collection in 1993, we still had no work by Francis Bacon, but now have two striking paintings from the beginning and end of his career (see pp.139 and 184). Similarly, in 1993 we had no works by Salvador Dalí, though we now have two superb oils and a number of prints and drawings (see pp.74–75).

The publication of this *Companion Guide* coincides with a further period of expansion for the Gallery as it approaches its fortieth anniversary in the year 2000. With the opening of The Dean Gallery, opposite the Gallery of Modern Art, we are almost doubling in size. This magnificent building, originally an orphanage designed by Thomas Hamilton in 1831, was offered to the National Galleries in 1994 by Lothian Region to house a generous gift by the Edinburgh-born sculptor Eduardo Paolozzi of a large collection of his work. We are also using The Dean to highlight our superb Dada and Surrealist collections, focusing in particular on artists' books and other material from the Penrose and Keiller archives which will be displayed in a specially designed library. Another significant feature of the conversion (by architects Terry Farrell & Partners) is a series of air-conditioned galleries for exhibitions of contemporary art.

The space gained by taking over The Dean means that more of our permanent collection than ever before will be publicly accessible. To mark the opening, we have purchased, jointly with the Tate Gallery – and made possible by an exception-ally generous grant from the NACF – one of the last masterpieces in the Penrose estate, Miró's *Head of a Catalan Peasant* 1925 (see frontispiece). In a kind of short-hand consisting of free-floating cursive and biomorphic shapes, Miró wittily depicts a bearded face surmounted by a distinctive red cap. The painting's radical move away from a Cubist treatment of space reflects Miró's recent involvement with the Surrealists, who were interested in dream imagery, myth and the uncon-scious. This new style of painting, which ignored conventions of gravity and which embraced chance, was to have an enormous influence on postwar art, in the United States as well as in Europe. Roland Penrose acquired the picture in 1937 and we are delighted that it has found a permanent home in Britain.

The following texts have been written by Patrick Elliott, Assistant Keeper at the Scottish National Gallery of Modern Art; we would also like to thank Michael Gormley for his assistance.

RICHARD CALVOCORESSI
Keeper, Scottish National Gallery of Modern Art

Edouard Vuillard 1868–1940

The Gallery owns six paintings by Vuillard, ranging in date from about 1892 to 1904: these are among the earliest works in the collection. Vuillard was born near Lyon, but the family moved to Paris in 1878. His father died when he was fifteen and thereafter his mother, who ran a small corset-making business from home, became the dominant influence in his life. *The Chat* is one of a series of paintings depicting the artist's mother and his sister, Marie. In these paintings, Vuillard generally depicts his mother as a large, expansive woman, at ease in her surroundings, while his sister appears awkward and submissive, sometimes literally blending into the wallpaper.

The women seen in profile in *Two Seamstresses in the Workroom* worked for Vuillard's mother. For a few years in the early 1890s Vuillard's paintings became so highly patterned that they verged on abstraction, and it is possible that his day-to-day contact with patterned materials informed his very intricate, decorative style of painting. *Two Seamstresses in the Workroom* was probably the first painting by Vuillard to enter a British collection. Vuillard gave it to the Scottish artist Charles Mackie and his wife Anne when they visited Paris in 1893. Anne later recorded in her diary: 'I remember Vuillard's little garret stacked with pictures and his kind command to take the picture we liked

The Chat (La Causette)
*c.*1892
Oil on canvas, 32.4 × 41.3
Presented by Sir Alexander Maitland in memory of his wife, Rosalind, 1960
GMA 2934

best … we were so afraid of being greedy that we took the smallest we could find but that picture is still a joy.'

Many of Vuillard's paintings of the turn of the century are small in scale and depict apparently mundane interiors or record uneventful episodes in domestic, middle-class life – subjects few other artists thought worthy of attention. His paintings of this type are often referred to as *intimiste*. The subject of *The Candlestick* is simply a bedside table placed against a wall, with a bag dangling down above it. Each element is given equal weight and the whole composition is unified by little dabs of paint. Vuillard often painted with a dry, sticky type of paint known as *colle* on soft brown cardboard, and would frequently leave some parts of the board unpainted, as in this picture, to form the neutral tone.

The Candlestick (Nature morte au bougeoir),
*c.*1900
Oil on millboard, 43.6 × 75.8
Presented by Mrs Isabel M. Traill 1979
GMA 2935

Two Seamstresses in the Workroom
(Deux ouvrières dans l'atelier de couture) 1893
Oil on millboard, 13.3 × 19.4
Purchased with assistance from the National Art
Collections Fund (Scottish Fund) and the National
Heritage Memorial Fund 1990
GMA 3583

Pierre Bonnard 1867–1947 · Lane at Vernonnet (Ruelle à Vernonnet) c.1912–14

Oil on canvas, 76 × 65.2
Purchased with funds given
by Mrs Charles Hope
Montagu Douglas Scott
1961
GMA 2932

Bonnard studied law but by the late 1880s had given this up for painting. In 1887 he enrolled at the Académie Julian, where he met Vuillard, Maurice Denis and Paul Sérusier. Taking their inspiration from Gauguin, the following year they formed the *Nabis* group (the name derives from the Hebrew word for 'Prophets').

In 1910 Bonnard rented a house called *Ma Roulotte* ('My Caravan') at Vernonnet, a village on the Seine, north west of Paris; he bought the house two years later. Monet was a close neighbour at Giverny. The two artists became good friends and there is sometimes an affinity between their work. By the time Bonnard moved to Vernonnet he had abandoned the dark tonalities of his early work for a vibrant palette of glowing purples, pinks, greens and yellows, as evident in this painting of about 1912–14. Bonnard later recalled: 'When my friends and I attempted to carry on, even go beyond, the work of the Impressionists we tried to surpass them in their naturalistic vision of colour. Art is not nature. We were more rigorous in our compositions, and found there was much more to be got out of colour.'

Pierre Bonnard 1867–1947
View of the River, Vernon (Echappée sur la rivière, Vernon) 1923

Like *Lane at Vernonnet*, this painting shows a view close to Bonnard's home. The river Seine is glimpsed through the trees and bushes while on the right three figures walking through the undergrowth can be distinguished. A fallen tree or branch is reduced to a slashed diagonal line which serves to unite the foreground and distance. As in many of Bonnard's mature landscapes, the rich colour and sensuous handling of paint create a feeling of warmth and luxuriance. Although he moved to the south of France in 1925, Bonnard kept the house at Vernonnet until the outbreak of war, returning there from time to time to paint.

Oil on canvas, 48.3 × 45.7
Presented by Sir Alexander Maitland in memory of his wife, Rosalind, 1960
GMA 2931

Pablo Picasso 1881–1973 · Mother and Child (Mère et enfant) 1902

The son of an artist, Picasso was born in Malaga, Spain, and studied at art school in Barcelona. He visited Paris in 1900 and after several extended stays settled there in 1904. From late 1901 until early 1904 he painted in a predominantly blue palette. The first of these 'Blue Period' works was painted after the suicide of a close friend, Carles Casagemas, whose death seems to have prompted Picasso to abandon his vivacious paintings of Bohemian Paris for more introspective, melancholy works.

Around autumn 1901, when Picasso was staying in Paris for the second time, he began making regular visits to a women's prison-hospital in the Saint-Lazare district of the city: there he found a plentiful supply of free models. The misery of these women, many of whom had babies or young children, seems to have struck a chord with the artist. He made several paintings of the inmates and their children, and continued this theme in Barcelona, where he stayed from January to October 1902. Mother and Child probably belongs to this Barcelona period.

Oil on paper laid on canvas, 40.5 × 33
Presented by Sir Alexander Maitland in memory of his wife, Rosalind, 1960
GMA 967

Georges Rouault 1871–1958 · Head c.1935–40

Oil on paper laid on canvas,
61.9 × 48.4
Presented by Sir Alexander
Maitland in memory of his
wife, Rosalind, 1960
GMA 968

Rouault was a contemporary of Matisse at the Ecole des Beaux-Arts in Paris, where both studied under the Symbolist painter Gustave Moreau. Rouault was a devout Catholic, and many of his paintings depict scenes from the life of Christ. He also made numerous paintings of female heads, often depicted in profile and painted in a heavy impasto with thick black outlines – a style indebted to his training as a maker of stained-glass windows. This composition closely relates to a project for a tapestry, hence the decorative border.

André Derain 1880–1954 · *Collioure* 1905

Oil on canvas, 60.2 × 73.5
Purchased 1973
GMA 1280

Derain was born near Paris and became friendly with Matisse and Vlaminck at the turn of the century. He spent the summer of 1905 with Matisse at Collioure in the south of France. In a letter to Vlaminck, Derain wrote enthusiastically of the 'blond, golden light that suppresses the shadows'. Inspired by the dazzling light, he and Matisse sought to recreate it by using pure, unmixed colours and loose brushwork. They returned to Paris in September and the following month exhibited their recent paintings at the Salon d'Automne; Vlaminck and others showed alongside them. In a review of the exhibition one critic likened a traditional sculpture shown in the same room to 'Donatello among the Fauves' (wild beasts). Since then the term 'Fauve' has been used to describe the brightly coloured paintings which Derain, Matisse and a few of their contemporaries made around 1905–08.

Chaïm Soutine 1893–1943 · *Les Gorges du Loup* c.1920–21

Soutine grew up in a small Jewish community in Lithuania where it was forbidden to draw or paint representational images. Against the wishes of his family, in 1910 he enrolled at art school in Vilna and three years later settled in Paris.

In 1919 Soutine moved to the village of Céret in the Pyrenees, close to the Spanish border (Braque, Picasso and Herbin had also worked there: see pp.28, 30 and 36). There he began to animate his landscape motifs with such frenzied brushwork that the trees and houses seem to lean in the wind. In 1918 he had visited the French Mediterranean coast with his friend Modigliani and he returned in the early 1920s, painting in and around Cagnes, near Nice. He executed about a dozen paintings of a nearby locality famous for its waterfalls, Les Gorges du Loup (literally 'The Throats of the Wolf'). For many years our painting has been titled *Les Gorges du Loup*, but it has recently been argued that it depicts a landscape in the Céret area.

Soutine's paintings are hard to date with accuracy, but this painting was made in about 1920–21, when the artist was living in desperate poverty. In the winter of 1922/23 Soutine was 'discovered' by the celebrated American collector Albert Barnes, who purchased a large number of his paintings, including this one.

Oil on canvas, 62.8×86.3
Purchased 1981
GMA 2312

Aristide Maillol 1861–1944 · *Eve with the Apple (Eve à la pomme)* 1899

Maillol was born at Banyuls-sur-Mer, a small town in the south of France, close to the Spanish border. He trained as a painter, associating with Vuillard and Bonnard (see pp.14–17), and also took up tapestry weaving, establishing his own workshop at Banyuls. However, the detailed work involved in weaving affected his eyesight, and by the late 1890s he was concentrating mainly on sculpture.

Already an experienced artist when he made his first sculptures, he swiftly arrived at a mature style. Although *Eve with the Apple* is among his earliest sculptures, it displays all the characteristics he would develop in his later work. Nearly all his sculptures are of female nudes, simply standing, sitting or kneeling. While Auguste Rodin (1840–1917), the dominant force in European sculpture at the turn of the century, had accentuated movement and expression, Maillol's art was concerned with balance, harmony and quiet restraint. It was the calm classicism of Maillol's work which distinguished him from nineteenth-century sculptors. After Rodin's death Maillol was widely regarded as his greatest successor, and his work exercised an enormous influence throughout Europe and the United States.

Bronze, 58.4 × 20.7 × 12
Purchased 1955
GMA 294

Emile-Antoine Bourdelle 1861–1929 · *The Virgin of Alsace (La Vierge d'Alsace)* 1919–21

Bronze, 250.2 × 84 × 58.5
Purchased 1930
GMA 2

From 1894 to 1908 Bourdelle, who was born at Montauban in the south of France, worked as an assistant to Auguste Rodin. He then began to establish his own reputation and after Rodin's death in 1917 was, with Maillol (see opposite), widely considered to be France's greatest living sculptor.

Bourdelle was a popular teacher, running a course at the Académie de la Grande Chaumière in Paris and also taking pupils at his own studio. The mother of one student owned potash mines in eastern France, and she vowed that should the mines survive the war with Germany she would erect a statue to the Virgin in thanksgiving. She died before the war was over but her son kept her promise and asked Bourdelle to make the statue.

The Gallery's version, which was exhibited in 1921, is an intermediary model for the full-size stone carving. Completed a year later, the six-metre-tall carving stands on a hill near Niederbruck in Alsace. The style of the work reflects Bourdelle's love of French Gothic sculpture. The figure of the Virgin is based upon the artist's wife Cléopatre and the child Jesus on his daughter Rhodia. Cléopatre was also a sculptor (she had been one of Bourdelle's students) and the head-scarf worn by the Virgin was inspired by one she used when carving, to keep the dust out of her hair.

Medardo Rosso 1858–1928 · Ecce Puer (Behold the Boy!) 1906

Rosso was one of the few sculptors who managed to suggest the space that surrounds a figure. His subjects seem to melt into the atmosphere, fusing with their environment. Rosso studied in Milan before moving to Paris, where he was based for much of the time from 1889. His work parallels that of his great contemporary, Auguste Rodin, in the impressionist modelling of form; in fact Rosso claimed that Rodin had stolen his ideas.

In the 1880s Rosso began to model his sculptures in clay, then cast them in wax. The wax had a similar translucency to skin and also gave his figures a dematerialised, ethereal quality. He also made his own bronze and plaster casts, sometimes painting the plasters to resemble wax: this is the case with the Gallery's cast of *Ecce Puer*. Although it was made in 1906 and Rosso died more than twenty years later, *Ecce Puer* is his last original sculpture. During the remaining years of his life he produced casts of earlier sculptures.

Ecce Puer (Behold the Boy!) is a portrait of Alfred William Mond. In 1906 Rosso was invited to London by Mond's father, Emil Mond (a member of a wealthy banking family) to make the young boy's bust. Legend has it that Rosso experienced great difficulty with the commission. Then, one evening, he was struck by the appearance of the boy as he peered through some curtains. Rosso chose to depict that fleeting moment and apparently finished the bust in a single sitting. When it was first exhibited, in Paris in 1906, the sculpture was titled *Impression of a Child*.

Plaster, gesso and varnish,
46.2 × 43 × 32
Purchased with funds from the estate of Miss J. L. Rose
1972
GMA 1274

Henri Matisse 1869–1954 · *Jeanette II* 1910

Though best known as a painter, Matisse was also a highly accomplished sculptor: he even taught sculpture at his own academy. His technique and approach were much indebted to Auguste Rodin. Rather than render skin as a smooth surface, Rodin modelled it to leave a rough texture which caught the light unevenly and gave his figures a lively, animated appearance. Matisse adopted a similar method.

Jeanette II belongs to a series of five busts of a young woman, Jeanne Vaderin, who was convalescing near Matisse's home at Issy-les-Moulineaux, south of Paris, in 1910. The first two busts were executed in front of the model and are quite naturalistic; the three later versions, made between 1911 and 1913, are progressively more stylised. *Jeanette I* is a slight, straightforward, and rather unremarkable bust. Using a separate cast of this, Matisse altered certain features to produce this second bust. The neck is eliminated, the hair transformed into a sculptural wave, and the nose pushed sideways to give the woman a lively, quizzical appearance. The cheeks are fuller, the lips pursed as if ready to speak, and the eyes have greater movement.

Bronze, 26.5 × 22.5 × 24
Purchased 1978
GMA 1995

Henri Matisse 1869–1954 · The Painting Lesson (La Leçon de peinture) 1919

Oil on canvas, 73.4 × 92.2
Bequeathed by Sir Alexander
Maitland 1965
GMA 929

During and immediately after the First World War, Matisse spent several long periods in Nice, in the south of France, staying at hotels or renting apartments near the sea front. Late in 1918 he took a room at the Hotel Méditerranée et de la Côte d'Azur, which looked directly onto the sea. He used the hotel as his base in Nice for the next three years.

The Painting Lesson is one of a series of about thirty paintings of the hotel room which contained, among other furnishings, a dressing table and decorative oval mirror. In the other works in the series the table is seen flush against a wall or near the window, with the mirror reflecting the interior of the room, but in our painting the mirror reflects the view seen through the window. The velvety black background serves to highlight the mirror and give an unusual, almost inverted sense of inside and outside space, in that the 'real' space of the room is dark and flattened while the flat mirror is alive with the reflected flowers, tree and sea.

The artist depicted to the left is presumably Matisse himself, while the young woman absorbed in her book is an eighteen-year-old model, Antoinette Arnoux. Soon after Matisse sold the picture it acquired the title The Painting Lesson, though it is not clear who named it. In any event, the picture and that title seem ill-matched and an alternative title, The Painting Session, has also been used in recent years.

Maurice Utrillo 1883–1955 · *La Place du Tertre c.1910*

Utrillo was born in Paris, the son of the artist Suzanne Valadon (she was also a model, appearing in works by Renoir and Degas among others). His father abandoned him but Miguel Utrillo, a Spanish writer and a friend of Valadon, adopted him in 1891. Although Maurice used his step-father's name he would always append a 'V' to his signature when he signed his paintings (or as in this case, when Valadon did, since she had much neater writing and signed many of her son's earlier works for him).

Utrillo was an alcoholic from an early age, and his mother encouraged him to paint as a remedial activity. Our painting depicts the Place du Tertre in Montmartre in the north of Paris. The building on the left housed a patisserie while the shop next to it sold tobacco and wine. The large building on the right of the square was a hotel.

Although Utrillo lived in Montmartre he usually preferred to paint from memory rather than in front of the motif, and he also copied from postcards: this may have been the case with this picture. Utrillo's work of 1910 to 1915 is widely regarded as his best and is termed his 'White Period'. He would often mix plaster with zinc white paint to give extra texture.

Oil on canvas, 49.5 × 72.4
Presented by Mr A. J. McNeill Reid in memory of his father, Alexander Reid, 1968: received 1972
GMA 1083

Georges Braque 1882–1963 · *The Candlestick (Le Bougeoir)* 1911

Oil on canvas, 46.2 × 38.2
Purchased 1976
GMA 1561

Braque was brought up in Le Havre where he trained as a painter and decorator. He moved to Paris in 1900, later becoming associated with the Fauves. Influenced by Cézanne, from 1907 he abandoned loose brushwork for a more structured, geometric style. Picasso's work developed in a similar way and the two friends' work is often difficult to tell apart during these years. Reviewing an exhibition of Braque's work in 1908 one critic wrote that he reduced everything to cubes and the derogatory term 'Cubism' soon came into being.

The Cubists rejected the convention that a painting is like a window on the world. Instead of choosing a fixed perspective they would paint a motif as if seen from different angles, showing several sides of an object in a single painting. Braque began to introduce lettering into his paintings in mid-1911 and *The Candlestick*, painted in the summer of 1911 when he was staying in Céret, in the Pyrenees, is a very early example of this type. Just as Cubist painting highlights the complex relationship that exists between the artist and the subject, so Braque's lettering questioned the relationship between words, pictures and the objects they represent. Instead of painting an object the artist could simply write its name on the canvas. Here, the lettering identifies the French-Catalan newspaper *L'Indépendant*, while the numbers refer to its price. Towards the top of the picture is a candle, which helps identify the shape below as a candle-stick. A simple clay pipe – the kind Braque smoked – lies to the centre right, and below it are a bobbin and a pair of scissors.

Pablo Picasso 1881–1973 · Guitar, Gas-Jet and Bottle (Guitare, bec à gaz, flacon) 1913

Oil, charcoal, tinted varnish
and grit on canvas,
70.4 × 55.3
Purchased 1982
GMA 2501

In the autumn of 1912 Picasso and Braque began sticking pieces of paper onto their drawings. Braque was the first to do this, applying a piece of wood-grained paper onto a drawing instead of trying to imitate wood with paint. This technique, known as *papier collé* (stuck paper), in turn affected the way Picasso and Braque painted. In *Guitar, Gas-Jet and Bottle* the vertical strips may look as if they have been stuck on, but they are in fact painted.

Picasso often introduced different techniques and styles into a single painting, as if to say that each was valid and no one approach was better than another. In this work, the gas-jet is drawn in charcoal in a straightforward manner. The stylised glass, represented as a circular top and bottom superimposed over a transparent container, is scratched into the thick white paint. The guitar is seen from both front and side angles, as if Picasso had moved around while he was painting it. The bottle also combines two perspectives, for we look down on the stopper and straight at the bottle itself. These different methods of representation call attention at once to flatness, spatial recession and the roving eye of the artist. Using these devices, Picasso underlines the active role of the artist in re-inventing, rather than making a copy of, the visible world.

John Richardson, Picasso's biographer, notes that the artist often pictured women in the curvaceous form of the guitar, and did so particularly with his new mistress, Eva. In this way he could depict her while keeping the tryst secret from his then partner, Fernande. Richardson sees the gas-lamp as a covert self-portrait, with its phallic form and incandescent flame.

Pablo Picasso 1881–1973 · Head (Tête) 1913

This work was made between March and June 1913 when Picasso was staying in Céret, in the Pyrenees. It is one of Picasso's most celebrated *papiers collés* (stuck papers), composed of strips of coloured paper arranged into a near abstract configuration, then given a figurative reference with the addition of a few charcoal lines. Picasso's use of collage had a profound affect on twentieth-century art.

Although it pre-dates the founding of Surrealism by more than a decade, *Head* has an important place in the history of Surrealism. It belonged to the leader of the Surrealist group, André Breton (see p.84), who bought it in 1923. He made it the first illustration in his book *Le Surréalisme et la peinture* (Surrealism and Painting), published in 1928. In desperate need of money, in 1936 Breton offered it to the British collector Roland Penrose (see p.124), but did so with a heavy heart: 'I am madly keen to keep this little picture which took me years to track down ... It is also the last Picasso I have, and I fear, that when I no longer have it I will feel poorer still.' The Surrealists admired Picasso for the liberties he took with form and for the way he almost magically transformed one object into another by the addition of a simple line.

Papiers collés with black chalk on card, 43.5 × 33
Purchased with assistance from the Heritage Lottery Fund and the National Art Collections Fund 1995
GMA 3890

Jacques Lipchitz 1891–1973 · *Seated Figure (Figure assise)* c.1916–17

Bronze, 78 × 29.2 × 29
Purchased 1968
GMA 1091

Lipchitz was born in Lithuania and moved to Paris in 1909. He was just one of a great many artists from eastern Europe who moved to Paris, then the world's art capital, in the early years of the twentieth century, forming what became known as the *Ecole de Paris* – the School of Paris.

Although a number of painters followed Braque and Picasso and adopted a Cubist style around 1909–10, a movement in Cubist sculpture only emerged a few years later. Lipchitz was to become perhaps the leading exponent of Cubist sculpture. By 1915 his sculptures had developed into almost abstract architectural forms and he later commented that this absence of any figurative content became a problem: 'In my Cubist sculpture I always wanted to retain the sense of organic life, of humanity.' Consequently, the following year he began to introduce figurative 'clues', while still retaining the austere Cubist language of cones, spheres and cubic forms. In *Seated Figure*, the small eye helps identify the sculpture as a human figure, and from this starting point we can detect the curves of the shoulder, arms and legs. The complex and dramatic construction of curved and linear forms is richly three-dimensional, encouraging the viewer to walk around the sculpture, rather than observe it from a fixed point.

Lyubov Popova 1889–1924 · *Painterly Architectonic* 1916

Popova was one of the most innovative of early twentieth-century Russian abstract artists. From 1912 to 1913 she was based in Paris, where she studied under the Cubist painter Jean Metzinger (see p.36). She began painting in a Cubist style at this date and on her return to Russia in 1914 exhibited and associated with Russian avant-garde groups. In 1916 her work became entirely abstract, consisting of coloured planes which seem to float in space. These paintings were much indebted to the work of the Russian artist Kasimir Malevich, who had reduced the Cubist style to a basic grammar of squares and rectangles: he called this new style 'Suprematism'.

Russian avant-garde art of this period was intimately connected with the Revolution and the forging of a new society. Popova saw abstract, 'constructive' art as a metaphor for construction in the modern industrial city, and referred to herself as an 'artist-engineer'. She and other avant-garde Russian artists saw themselves as making a new kind of art fit for a brave new world.

Oil on board, 59.4 × 39.4
Purchased 1979
GMA 2080

Fernand Léger 1881–1955 · *Woman and Still Life (Femme et nature morte)* 1921

Born in Normandy, Léger moved to Paris in 1902. Early in his career he was apprenticed to an architect. His first Cubist paintings date from 1909. Of all the Cubist artists, Léger was the one most inspired by modern machinery and industrial forms. For him, machines had a dual appeal: they were beautiful, with their crisp functional forms, and they also offered the hope for a new utopian order, in which workers would be freed from dull, repetitive tasks.

Léger introduced mechanical elements into his paintings not by copying machines but by constructing his compositions with the rigour and clarity of an engineer. The grid-like structures in his paintings may also reflect the influence of Mondrian (see p.38), whose work he first saw in 1920. Between 1920 and 1921 Léger made a series of paintings of a reclining nude

woman and a still life. Some versions include a second woman standing in the centre-foreground, next to a table with a still life, while others feature a reclining nude and a still life in which a tall lamp takes the place of the standing woman. In our painting a vestige of the standing woman / lamp remains, though these elements have been transformed into a disc which connects to the still life in the fore-ground. The series reached its culmination in a large painting of three women called *Le Grand déjeuner* (Museum of Modern Art, New York).

Oil on canvas, 65.5 × 92
Purchased 1965
GMA 962

Sonia Delaunay 1885–1979 with Blaise Cendrars 1887–1961 · *The Trans-Siberian Prose (La Prose du transsibérien et de la petite Jehanne de France)* 1913

Pochoir and text on paper,
199 × 35.5
Purchased 1980
GMA 2199

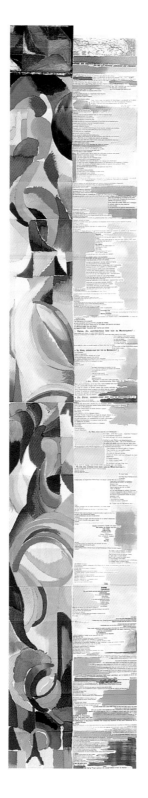

Sonia Terk was born in the Ukraine and settled in Paris in 1905, marrying the artist Robert Delaunay (see opposite) five years later. The couple became leading practitioners of what became known as 'Simultanism', an offshoot of Cubism and Futurism. They sought to distil a multitude of different 'modern' experiences and present them simultaneously in a single picture. Inventions such as the car, aeroplane, cinema and telephone had changed the way people experienced the world, and artists and writers sought to capture that change in their work.

The Trans-Siberian Prose, written by the poet Blaise Cendrars and accompanied by Delaunay's abstract composition, was described as 'the first simultanist book'. The poem is a semi-autobiographical, semi-fictional account of a train journey across Russia, but it is particularly concerned with Cendrars' thoughts as they flash backward and forward, evoking memories of Paris and his love for a young French prostitute. Instead of illustrating the text, Delaunay wanted to find a visual equivalent for the way it evokes patterns of thought. At the foot of the text is the only illustrative element, the Eiffel Tower, which Sonia and Robert Delaunay regarded as the archetypal emblem of modernity.

The 'book' comprises four joined sheets of paper folded into a hand-painted wallet. An edition of 150 had been envisaged (laid end to end, they would have equalled the height of the Eiffel Tower), but only about sixty were made. Although each copy looks like an original painting, the colours were in fact applied through a stencil (*pochoir*), making each example virtually identical.

Oil and tempera on canvas,
146.8 × 114.2
Purchased 1985
GMA 2942

In 1912 Delaunay began the first of several versions of *The Cardiff Team*. He seems to have painted two other versions before the First World War, and two more between 1922 and 1923. The motif derived from a newspaper photograph of a Cardiff-Paris rugby match showing players jumping for the ball. Delaunay added Paris's famous Ferris wheel and an 'Astra' bill-board, which refers to an aircraft construction company. The letters on the hoarding to the right derive from the artist's own name. The Eiffel Tower, that symbol of modernity, features in many of Delaunay's paintings and is here seen emerging above the fragment of his name. Sport was also a 'modern' subject since rugby and football only began to gain in popularity in the 1890s and early 1900s as leisure time increased. (During the War Delaunay and Diaghilev even collaborated on a project for a ballet based on the theme of rugby or football.) Delaunay wrote about another version of *The Cardiff Team*: 'The surface of the painting is living and simultaneous. The whole picture is a unity of rhythms. Modern elements: the poster, the Big Wheel. The Eiffel Tower was part of a football game, bodies tangled up with life.'

Auguste Herbin 1882–1960 and Jean Metzinger 1883–1956

Auguste Herbin
Composition 1919
Oil on canvas, 73 × 91.5
Bequeathed by Gabrielle Keiller 1995
GMA 3986

Jean Metzinger
Landscape (Paysage) c.1921
Oil on canvas, 60 x 81.3
Purchased 1970
GMA 1111

Although Picasso and Braque 'invented' Cubism, they chose not to show at the major Paris exhibitions, and so their followers – who exhibited widely and were more vocal – came to be seen as the public face of the new movement. Alongside Gleizes, Delaunay and Le Fauconnier, Herbin and Metzinger were among the leading members of this group of artists who are sometimes referred to as the 'Salon Cubists'. They first attracted attention at the Salon exhibitions of 1911 and by the outbreak of war constituted a significant if fragmented group.

Metzinger and Herbin both painted in the Fauvist style before adopting the Cubist idiom of geometric patterning and angular planes around 1910–12. Metzinger was one of the first artists to follow the example of Braque and Picasso, though he is perhaps still best known for the influential book on Cubism which he co-wrote in 1912. Herbin's *Composition* was painted in the small French town of Céret, in the Pyrenees, where Picasso and a number of the Cubist artists regularly stayed (Herbin lived there from 1918 to 1920). Unified by decorative forms which rhyme and echo across the canvas, *Composition* depicts a stylised female figure on the right and landscape elements on the left, separated by what is perhaps a curtain.

Julio González 1876–1942 · Harlequin (L'Arlequin) c.1929–30

Bronze,
40.8 × 27.5 × 29.5
Purchased 1972
GMA 1259

González was born in Barcelona, where his father and grandfather were skilled jewellers and metalworkers. During his apprenticeship in his father's workshop he learned the techniques of cutting, soldering and forging metals. Artistic metalwork had a long tradition in Spain where some of the finest European armour and weaponry had been produced, and it is no accident that the leading early twentieth-century exponents of welded metal and forged iron sculpture were Spanish.

In 1900 the González family moved to Paris where Julio renewed his acquaintance with Picasso, an old friend from Barcelona. He continued making decorative metalwork and only in the late 1920s did he begin to make large sculptures. González had learned the technique of oxyacetylene welding at a car factory near Paris, so when Picasso decided to make some large forged iron sculptures, he went to his friend for help: this collaboration lasted from 1928 to 1931. Inspired by Picasso, González began making his own forged iron sculptures, one of the earliest of which is *Harlequin*. The head and the harlequin's patterned costume are re-created but the sculpture works principally in sculptural terms, as an assembly of solids and voids, volumes and flat planes. González is regarded as the pioneer of this method, which challenges traditional sculpture techniques such as modelling in clay or carving in stone. The original iron version of *Harlequin* is in the Kunsthaus in Zurich; the Gallery's version is a posthumous bronze cast.

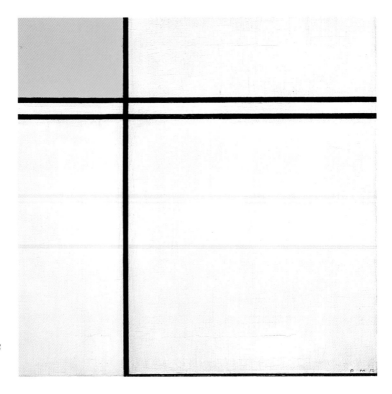

Oil on canvas, 45.3 × 45.3
Purchased 1982
GMA 2502

Mondrian was the leading artist of the De Stijl ('the style') movement, a group of Dutch artists advocating a rigorously spare form of geometric, abstract art. Although Mondrian's paintings are extremely pure and simple, they develop from a complex set of ideas. He was strongly influenced by, and was a member of, the mystical, quasi-religious Theosophical group. Theosophists championed the spiritual above the material, and one branch of the movement saw existence in terms of polarities, of male and female, positive and negative, horizontal and vertical. This notion is embodied in Mondrian's grid paintings in which opposites are united in balanced harmony.

Mondrian's paintings have a machine-like rigour but they grew out of his study of natural forms, again an important source for Theosophists. For example, a series of studies of tree branches evolved into a criss-cross configuration of lines between 1909 and 1913. Another important influence was Cubism.

Composition is one of the earliest of Mondrian's so-called 'tram-line' paintings. Before 1932 he had used single transecting lines but he then began pairing them in order to achieve a sense of optical movement. He also began to carry the coloured patches over the edge of the canvas. This device suggested that the painting extended beyond the boundaries of the canvas itself and into the real space of the room in which it hung.

The painting formerly belonged to Winifred Nicholson (see p.111) who acquired it directly from Mondrian when he was living in London in the late 1930s.

Oil on canvas,
104.8 × 104.8
Purchased 1980
GMA 2148

Vordemberge-Gildewart belonged to the generation of artists which reached maturity in the 1920s and embarked almost immediately on abstract painting, instead of arriving at abstraction through a process of reduction – as Picasso, Braque, Kandinsky and Mondrian had done.

Born in Germany, Vordemberge-Gildewart studied in Hanover and became a close friend of Kurt Schwitters (see p.58), who also lived there. From 1925 he had close ties with the Dutch De Stijl group. Although his paintings resemble Mondrian's, the approaches of the two artists were entirely different, Mondrian's art evolving from deeply held spiritual beliefs, while Vordemberge-Gildewart shunned all association with symbol and metaphor. He argued that art represented nothing but itself, advocating what he called 'Absolute Art': 'The spiritual in art does not exist … For absolute art, so-called content and object are totally impossible.' This austere approach was reflected in the titles of his paintings which are simply numerical.

El Lissitzky 1890–1941 · Proun. 1st Kestner Portfolio (1° Kestnermappe Proun) 1923

Portfolio of six lithographs, two with collage, each
60 × 44
Purchased 1983
GMA 2767

Like his fellow Russian artists Jawlensky and Kandinsky (see pp.48 and 54), El Lissitzky studied in Germany, attending courses on engineering and architecture in Darmstadt. At the outbreak of war he returned to Russia. In 1919 he met the Suprematist artist Kasimir Malevich, who had reduced painting to simple but dynamic squares and rectangles. Lissitzky adapted this approach to architectural projects, developing the 'Proun' which he called 'an interchange station between painting and architecture.' These works, and the new geometric abstract art which became so popular in Russia at the time of the Revolution, responded to the new political landscape and to the utopian ideals that it engendered. Lissitzky exclaimed that 'Our lives are now being built on a new communist foundation ... On such a foundation – thanks to the Prouns – monolithic communist towns will be built, in which the inhabitants of the world will live.' The clarity, precision and formal strength of his art were intended as metaphors for the new socialist order.

Following a spell teaching architecture in Moscow, Lissitzky moved back to Germany in 1922. Through Kurt

Schwitters (see p.58), he was offered an exhibition by the Kestner Gesellschaft in Hanover early in 1923. Founded during the war, the Kestner was an independent society which arranged exhibitions of contemporary art. Encouraged by the success of the exhibition, the gallery commissioned Lissitzky to make this suite of lithographic prints as New Year gifts for the society's members. The cover and three of the lithographs are illustrated here.

Portfolio Cover

László Moholy-Nagy 1895–1946 · Sil I 1933

Moholy-Nagy was born in Hungary and in 1921 moved to Berlin via Vienna. From 1923 to 1928 he taught at the Bauhaus, at that time the most advanced art school in Europe. Contrary to traditional teaching practice, the courses dealt with matters such as texture, movement, light, film and photography.

In the early 1920s Moholy-Nagy was strongly influenced by the work of the Russian Suprematists (see opposite and p.32). Their paintings were composed of abstract geometric forms which mirrored the pioneer spirit of the new machine age and suggested clarity, construction and rational thought. Extending this association with the modern, in the mid-1920s Moholy-Nagy abandoned traditional easel painting and began to paint on aluminium, plastic, celluloid and other new industrial materials. Aluminium had associations with new technology and also satisfied Moholy-Nagy's desire to, as he put it, 'paint with light', since it was reflective. At the Bauhaus his courses had included metalwork and photography, itself an art concerned with capturing reflected light rays. He wrote that 'Experiments with painting on highly polished black panels or coloured transparent or translucent plates produce strange optical effects: it looks as though the colour were *floating* almost without material effect in a space in front of the plane to which it is in fact applied.'

In 1933 Moholy-Nagy painted at least three works on a new type of aluminium called silberit: the Gallery's painting is the first of these, hence the title.

Oil and incised lines on silberit, 50 × 20
Purchased 1977
GMA 1663

Gustav Klimt 1862–1918 · Pregnant Woman with Man (Schwangere mit Mann nach links) c.1903–04

Klimt was the leading artist of the Vienna Secession, a group famous for its love of stylised forms and sinuous ornament. He was not a prolific painter but he did make thousands of drawings. Although this drawing and a number of related sketches have been called studies for the painting *Hope I* (*Hoffnung I*) of 1903, there are significant differences and it may not have been made with any particular painting in mind. Klimt tended to make rapid sketches of his models as they walked about the studio, and he would then use these drawings as the basis for his compositions. His subject matter of naked women in erotic poses aroused much controversy during his lifetime. *Hope I*, which features a pregnant woman, achieved particular notoriety.

Klimt's fascination with the great subjects of human existence – birth, love, suffering and death – is part of a general Symbolist movement in European art which emerged in the 1880s and is a particular feature of northern European art. Munch and Hodler (see pp.46 and 52) were similarly concerned with such themes.

Black chalk on paper,
44.7 × 30.6
Purchased 1985
GMA 2946

Oskar Kokoschka 1886–1980

Kokoschka grew up in Vienna. His early work, which is predominantly graphic, shows the influence of Klimt and the Vienna Secession; but in *Die traümenden Knaben*, a 'fairy tale' with text and images by Kokoschka, first published in 1908, the jagged rhythms, distorted figures and folk-art style suggest a move away from Secessionist decoration towards Expressionism.

From about 1910 to 1914 Kokoschka painted a remarkable series of portraits which expose the nervous inner life of his sitters. One of his finest portrait drawings of this period is of Alma Mahler (1879–1964). The beautiful daughter of the Austrian landscape painter Emil Jakob Schindler, Mahler was muse to some of the great early twentieth-century artists. Klimt fell in love with her but was ultimately spurned; the composer Gustav Mahler was her first husband (they married in 1902); Kokoschka was her lover after Mahler's death; and following Kokoschka's enlistment in the Imperial Cavalry in 1915, she married the architect Walter Gropius.

Kokoschka met Alma Mahler in April 1912 and they immediately embarked upon a turbulent love affair. He painted several portraits of her and a celebrated oil, *The Tempest*, which depicts the couple together on a stormy sea. This is a study for one of the lithographs in *Columbus in Chains*, a book which reflects the tensions in their relationship.

The Dreaming Boys (Die traümenden Knaben) 1908
Book with eleven lithographs, 24.1 × 29.5
Purchased 1990
GMA 3552

Alma Mahler c.1913
Black chalk on paper, 39.2 × 31.5
Purchased 1987
GMA 3037

Ernst Ludwig Kirchner 1880–1938 · Japanese Theatre (Japanisches Theater) c.1909

Kirchner was the leading member of the *Brücke* (Bridge) group, which was formed in Dresden in 1905. The original members were Kirchner, Heckel, Bleyl and Schmidt-Rotluff, and others including Emil Nolde (see p.49) joined later. The name *Die Brücke* was chosen to suggest the links or 'bridges' which connected the artists of the group, but it also stood for the bridges they hoped to build between art and life, artist and public, decorative and fine art, past and future.

At first the members of the group were strongly influenced by Van Gogh's work, which featured in several exhibitions held in Dresden from 1905. They also owed much to Gauguin and his espousal of primitivism. After about 1908 the work of the *Brücke* artists loosened up considerably, partly due to the influence of French Fauve painting. *Japanese Theatre* is among the first of Kirchner's works in this new, raw style. It is also among his first paintings to depict a stage scene: the theatre, cabaret and circus became favourite themes of the *Brücke* artists. Kirchner depicted a broad range of performers, from wrestlers and acrobats to exotic Eastern and African dancers. Such acts became popular in the Bohemian bars and theatres of Germany in the early years of the century, partly due to Germany's colonial expansion.

Japanese Theatre shows actors from a Japanese theatre company performing at Dresden's Albert Theatre. The exact nature and spatial arrangement of the scene is ambiguous. The two figures in the foreground seem to occupy the front edge of the set, and are separated from the third figure by a curtain. The woman on the left holds what may be a dagger. The artist's unusual viewpoint, looking down on the actors from a side angle, suggests that he may have seen the play from a theatre box.

In about 1924 Kirchner reversed the canvas and painted another work on the back. The standing man is probably a self-portrait. The totemic, primitivist sculpture, shown on the left, is probably by Kirchner himself.

Verso: Interior with Nude Woman and Man
Oil on canvas, 113.7 × 113.7
Purchased 1965
GMA 911

Oil on canvas, 113.7 × 113.7
Purchased 1965
GMA 911

Edvard Munch 1863–1944 · *The Sick Girl (Das kranke Mädchen)* 1896

Colour lithograph on paper,
42.1 × 56.3
Purchased 1981
GMA 2309

This celebrated print relates to Munch's eldest sister, Sophie, and to her death of tuberculosis in 1877, aged just fifteen. Munch made several paintings of the subject, as well as a group of lithographs executed twenty years after the event. It is not an exact portrayal of the death-bed scene: a model actually posed for the work. The painted versions belong to *The Frieze of Life*, a series of heavily symbolic images which Munch made in the 1890s and which deal with the themes of life, love and death. However, the lithograph is based upon an earlier painting, dating from 1885–86. In the print Munch focuses on the upper section of the painting which depicts the girl in bed, propped up against a large pillow (the mother figure to her side is eliminated here).

The Sick Child is Munch's first colour lithograph and he regarded it as his most important print. Lithographs are made by drawing with a waxy crayon on a special stone slab, each colour requiring a separate stone. It was made in Paris, where Munch stayed for several months in 1896. In Paris he experimented with colour lithography at the celebrated printmaking workshop of Auguste Clot. For this print Munch worked on a large number of stones, printing them in different combinations to produce a variety of colour and image permutations.

Ernst Ludwig Kirchner 1880–1938 · White Dancer in a Cabaret (Weisse Tänzerin in kleinem Variété) 1914

Lithograph on paper,
65.2 × 50.4
Purchased 1984
GMA 2924

Kirchner's father worked in paper manufacture and had a keen interest in art. With his encouragement, Ernst Ludwig made prints and drawings from an early age. Kirchner was by far the most prolific of the German Expressionist printmakers, producing more than 2000 prints in woodcut, etching and lithography.

From about 1908, many of the German *Brücke* artists depicted cabaret, theatre and circus scenes in their paintings and prints (see pp.44–45). Such acts appealed because they were simultaneously urban and exotic. The *Brücke* artists were keen to be seen to be modern and they therefore selected city-based subjects; but they also loved the primitive and the erotic. This rare lithograph (only one other impression of this second, final state is known), depicts a group of men seated at a table, their hats and coats hung up on the wall. The dancer is so close to them that they seem to have to lean back to avoid her high kick.

Oil on millboard laid on plywood, 52.2 × 50.2
Purchased 1964
GMA 896

Jawlensky was born in Russia, and started out on a military career. He began his art studies comparatively late, in his mid-twenties, and in 1896 left the army and went to Munich where he enrolled at art school. Another Russian artist, Wassily Kandinsky (see p.54), was a fellow student, and the two became great friends. In 1905 Jawlensky spent some time in France, where he was influenced by the work of Gauguin, Van Gogh and the Fauves. He showed several paintings at the famous Salon d'Automne exhibition of 1905, when the Fauves burst onto the scene with such force. The violent colours and broad brushstrokes seen in *Head of a Woman* may be compared with paintings by Derain (see p.20).

Jawlensky's painting achieved maturity in 1911. He later wrote that 'that summer meant a great step forward in my art … My forms were very strongly coloured in Prussian blue and came with tremendous inner ecstasy … It was in these years, up to 1914, just before the war, that I painted my most powerful works.' The great majority of Jawlensky's works are portraits and heads of women, and in a sense he was continuing the great tradition of Russian icon painting. His later work became increasingly stylised, with the female head being reduced to a few schematic forms and lines.

Emil Nolde 1867–1956 · Head (Kopf) 1913

Emil Hansen was born in Nolde, a town which is now just on the Danish side of the Danish-German border. He changed his name to Nolde when he was in his late thirties. For a brief period, from 1906 to 1908, he was a member of the Brücke group (see p.44). Like Kirchner and the other members of the group Nolde loved primitive art and from about 1911 he made regular visits to the Ethnographic Museum in Berlin, producing watercolours of the exhibits. These served as the basis for a series of imaginative paintings in which tribal artefacts are juxtaposed in such a way that they seem to come to life in interior and landscape settings.

When he was offered the chance to go to New Guinea on an official expedition, Nolde grasped the opportunity, even though he had to pay his own way. He left Germany in October 1913 and returned nearly a year later. In a list of his own works Nolde dated this Head to 1913, and it has been thought that it was painted on the trip. However, this is unlikely, for the painting was probably exhibited in Germany at the beginning of 1914 while Nolde was still away. It is more likely that it was painted shortly before his departure and stands as a kind of rehearsal for the type of painting he anticipated making on the trip.

Oil on canvas, 77.5 × 67.3
Purchased 1968
GMA 1082

Mikhail Larionov 1881–1964 · *Soldier in a Wood* c.1911

Oil on canvas, 84.5 × 91.4
Purchased with funds given
by two anonymous donors
1962
GMA 799

Larionov studied in Moscow, where in 1900 he met fellow student Natalya Goncharova (see opposite), who would become his lifelong companion. The chronology of their early work, and of much early twentieth-century Russian art, is difficult to establish. This painting was discovered in a locked attic in Larionov's Paris flat in about 1960 (he and Goncharova had settled in Paris in 1917) and was purchased directly from the artist in 1962. It was probably painted around 1911 when Larionov was doing his military service.

Larionov is the artist most closely identified with the Russian Neo-Primitivist movement, which emerged around 1909–10. Although Russian artists benefited greatly from their contacts with France (Larionov first visited Paris in 1906), many were equally inspired by local artistic forms, such as icon painting, folk-art and the popular woodblock prints known as *lubok*. In *Soldier in a Wood* we see elements from these kinds of sources, in the flattened, simplified design, in the bold brushwork and in the deliberately naïve manner of representation.

Natalya Goncharova 1881–1962 · *Rabbi with Cat c.*1912

For many years this painting was known as *Monk with Cat*, though the figure is in fact a Rabbi. The two men carrying sacks in the background are Jews fleeing a pogrom; the Hand of God is seen in the top left corner, blessing the Rabbi. The Rabbi is perhaps stroking the cat for the last time before he too departs. The picture is clearly indebted to Russian icons, so much so that we may see an analogy between the Rabbi and cat and the Virgin and Child. As such, the painting delivers a poignant message about compassion, suffering and religious intolerance.

Goncharova was the lifelong companion of Larionov. Born near Tula, she studied painting in Moscow and, with Larionov, moved to Paris in 1917. She worked closely with Diaghilev and for other ballet and theatre companies.

Oil on canvas, 100.2 × 92
Purchased with funds given by two anonymous donors
1962
GMA 796

Ferdinand Hodler 1853–1918 · Lake Thun and the Stockhorn Mountains (Thunersee mit Stockhornkette) 1910

Oil on canvas, 83 × 105.4
Purchased 1975
GMA 1523

Hodler was born in Bern, Switzerland. His parents died when he was young and his brothers and sister also died at an early age. Death was a popular theme among the Symbolist artists of the 1880s and 1890s – for example Munch and Klimt – and not surprisingly it is one of the main themes in Hodler's art.

A deeply religious artist, Hodler was very conscious of the symmetry in the life cycle of birth and death and saw symmetry in nature as an extension of this. Developing a theory he called Parallelism, Hodler sought to express the underlying order and unity in the natural world through symmetry of composition (the theoretical reasoning behind Mondrian's work was similar: see p.38). Many of his late landscapes are of the Lake Thun area, near Bern, with the mountain ranges rising into a peak in the middle and finding their mirrored reflection in the still water. He saw the horizontal line as symbolic of death – he made a remarkable series of paintings of both his dying wife, and subsequently of his dying lover, stretched out horizontally across the centre of the canvas – and it is the flat, horizontal line which tends to dominate these late landscapes. Hodler even wrote about the central mountain peaks in these landscapes as representing the soul of his beloved. Nature, life, love and death are thus unified in this majestic landscape.

Lyonel Feininger 1871–1956 · *Gelmeroda III* 1913

Feininger was born in New York and moved to Germany at the age of sixteen. He first drew the church at Gelmeroda, a small village near Weimar, in 1906. It became a recurrent motif in his work, featuring in numerous drawings and prints and in thirteen oil paintings ranging in date from 1913 to 1936. In 1913 Feininger wrote to a friend about the area: 'Weimar is infinitely dear to me … The villages – there must be nearly a hundred in the vicinity – are wonderful. The architecture (you know how much I depend upon it) is just to my liking. There are some church steeples in God-forsaken villages which belong to the most mystical achievements of so-called civilised man.'

In 1911 Feininger visited Paris and saw Cubist paintings for the first time, and thereafter he began to use a grid-like structure in his own paintings. Although the church at Gelmeroda carried a symbolic meaning in his work, its architectural form also provided the ideal motif for an artist interested in geometric compositions. The first two Gelmeroda paintings, also dating from 1913, are very dynamic in appearance, featuring a leaning spire cut up by sharp Cubist planes. In this third version Feininger produced a more austere, balanced composition.

Oil on canvas, 100.5 × 80
Purchased 1985
GMA 2951

Wassily Kandinsky 1866–1944 · Small Worlds (Kleine Welten) 1922

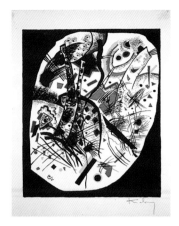

Portfolio of twelve prints,
46 × 35.5 (portfolio size)
Purchased with assistance
from the National Heritage
Memorial Fund and the
National Art Collections
Fund 1994
GMA A35.RPL1–13

This rare, complete set of twelve prints in their original portfolio, comprises four colour lithographs, four wood-cuts – colour alternating with black and white – and four drypoints. The cover and three of the prints are illustrated here. In the accompanying introduction Kandinsky emphasised the different character of his chosen media (the different printing tech-niques are carried out on stone, wood and copper) and the importance of the alternation between colour and black and white. He concluded: 'In all twelve cases, each of the "Small Worlds" adopts, in line or patch, its own necessary language.'

Born in Moscow, Kandinsky studied in Munich from 1897 and spent most of the next twenty years there, becoming one of the first exponents of abstract art as well as one of its leading theorists. He then spent several years in Moscow before returning to Germany in 1921 and taking a teaching post at the Weimar Bauhaus art school the following year (Feininger and Klee were fellow members of staff: see p.53 and opposite). *Small Worlds* dates from Kandinsky's first months at the Bauhaus. It contains a mixture of the free, linear, apparently automatic compositions of his Munich years, and the more geometric, 'constructive' forms of his Russian years (compare, for example, with Popova's work: p.32). Much of the imagery is based on landscape and seascape motifs, often of an apocalyptic nature. Developed, refined and schematised over a twenty-year period, these motifs appear in the prints as seemingly abstract configurations of line and colour.

Portfolio Cover

Paul Klee 1879–1940 · *Ghost of a Genius (Gespenst eines Genies)* 1922

Born near Bern in Switzerland, Klee studied in Munich, where Kandinsky and Jawlensky were already settled. Kandinsky and Klee became fellow teachers at the Weimar Bauhaus in the 1920s. This work may be a self-portrait (Klee had very large eyes, a domed head and a closely cropped beard). He made many puppets for his son, and this figure, with its arms flopping down and tilted head, may have been inspired by a puppet.

The technique of oil transfer, employed here, involves covering a sheet of thin paper with a special oil paint, placing a sheet of paper on it, and then drawing on the top sheet with a sharp instrument so that the paint transfers onto it. This home-made carbon-copy process gives an effect halfway between drawing and printing, and produces appealing smudges where the artist's hand has rested on the paper. He could also trace preliminary drawings this way, and in doing so keep a record of the works he had done. Our work seems to have been traced from a pen drawing now in the Norton Simon Museum in Pasadena, then coloured in with watercolour.

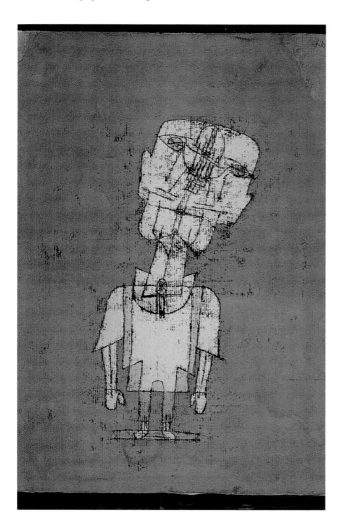

Oil transfer and watercolour on paper laid on card, 50 × 35.4
Purchased 1979
GMA 2106

Max Beckmann 1884–1950 · *Hell (Die Hölle)* 1919

Portfolio of eleven lithographs, each 87 × 61 Purchased 1981
GMA 2465

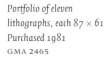

Beckmann was born in Leipzig. He studied in Weimar and Paris before settling in Berlin. At the outbreak of war he volunteered for the medical corps, but in 1915 he suffered a nervous breakdown and was later discharged. At about this time he moved away from Impressionism and adopted a more angular style. Though not involved with politics, much of his work deals with political and social change in Germany.

The narrative print cycle, issued in book or portfolio form, had a strong tradition in Germany. *Hell* is the most important of several portfolios made by Beckmann. Following the abdication of the Kaiser and the armistice in November 1918, revolutions broke out in several German cities. These were brutally suppressed by the army. In *Hell*, Beckmann chronicles this period of lawlessness, social decay and misery. The portfolio consists of a title-page and ten lithographs, two of which are illustrated here. The title-page bears a self-portrait of the artist sitting in a fairground booth. A text

below invites us to follow him on a tour of the city: 'We ask our esteemed public to step forward. You will not be bored for ten minutes. Anyone who is not delighted gets his money back.' *The Way Home* (illustrated above left) is the first of the ten prints. It depicts Beckmann himself, greeting a disfigured soldier who has returned from the war. In the following prints we are introduced to a strange cast of characters – bankers, prostitutes, cripples, revolutionaries and beggars. Beckmann portrays Berlin as a violent hell on earth. Several of the prints refer to the repression of the left-wing Spartacist League and to the brutal murder of their leaders. *The Last Ones* (illustrated above right) the ninth of the ten prints, depicts a small group of revolutionaries making their last stand against the forces of government.

George Grosz 1893–1959 · Toads of Property (Die Besitzkröten) 1920

With Otto Dix (see p.62), Grosz is the best-known of the political artist-satirists who flourished in Germany after the First World War. Owing to illness he was unfit for war service and could instead watch from the sidelines as invalids and cripples returned from the Front while a few industrialists made their fortunes. *Toads of Property* was one of nine drawings by Grosz reproduced in *The Robbers (Die Räuber)* a suite of lithographs published in 1922. Each print was accompanied by a quotation from Schiller's play *The Robbers*. Our work carried the following text: 'Under my rule it shall be brought to pass, that potatoes and small-beer shall be considered a holiday treat; and woe to him who meets my eye with the audacious front of health. Haggard want, and crouching fear, are my insignia; and in this livery will I clothe ye'.

In the catalogue of his exhibition in Hanover in 1922, Grosz, who was a member of the Communist party, commented: 'Humanity has created an evil system – a top and bottom. A few make millions while countless thousands have barely enough to survive ... The purpose of my work is ... to reveal to the oppressed the true faces of their rulers.' However, it has often been noted that Grosz harboured bourgeois ambitions and seemed to caricature the poor as much as he did the rich.

Pen and ink on paper,
52.7 × 41.1
Purchased 1979
GMA 2102

Kurt Schwitters 1887–1948

Mz.299 1921
Collage on paper, 20 × 16
Bequeathed by Gabrielle
Keiller 1995
GMA 4081

Untitled (Relief with Red
Pyramid)
(Ohne Titel (Relief mit
roter Pyramide))
c.1923–25
Oil on wood relief on
plywood, 60 × 50.2
Purchased 1979
GMA 2077

Based in Hanover, Schwitters was a leading German Dadaist. In 1919 he began composing collages and assemblages from junk materials such as wood, scraps of paper and everyday ephemera. He called these works *Merz*, a term derived from the cut-up letterhead of a bank called 'Kommerz und Privatbank' (the association of rubbish with banks was deliberately ironic). *Mz.299* (the 299th of the series) is an early and typical example of these collages. From 1923 to 1924 Schwitters published a review called *Merz*. He later wrote: 'I could not, in fact, see any reason why one should not use the old tickets, driftwood, cloakroom numbers, wires and parts of wheels, buttons and old lumber out of junkrooms and rubbish heaps as materials for paintings as well as the colours that were produced in factories.'

Although *Relief with Red Pyramid* appears to be an abstract composition, it probably refers to the discovery in 1922 of the tomb of Tutankhamun, an event which had a major and immediate impact in the art-world. The tall figures mimic the stylised profiles found in Egyptian art. This relief could be seen as a tongue-in-cheek reworking of the Constructivist style of artists like Popova (see p.32).

Hannah Höch 1889–1960 · From the Collection: From an Ethnographic Museum (Aus der Sammlung: Aus einem ethnographischen Museum) 1929

Born in Gotha, Höch met the Dada artist Raoul Hausmann in 1915 and through him became involved with the Berlin Dada group. Although she did paint, she is best known for her satirical and disturbing photomontages. This work is from a series of some seventeen photomontages executed between 1924 and 1930 and given the generic title *From an Ethnographic Museum*. They all incorporate reproductions of African tribal sculpture coupled mainly with photographs from contemporary fashion magazines. The meeting of the two different cultures is deliberately enigmatic, creating weird hybrid figures.

The geometric elements around the figure recall the work of Mondrian and the *De Stijl* group. Höch was associated with this group, and this collage formerly belonged to one of its members, Friedrich Vordemberge-Gildewart (see p.39). Höch was also closely associated with Kurt Schwitters (see opposite), with whom she collaborated on several *Merz* projects.

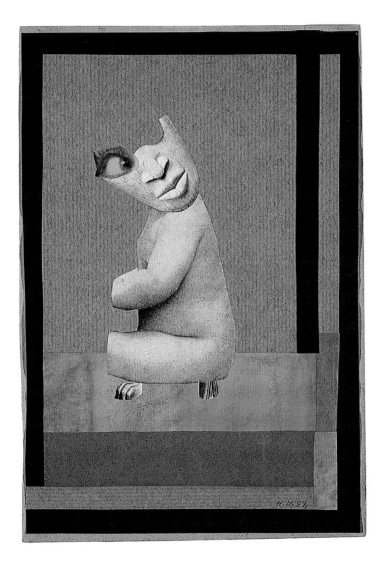

Collage and gouache on paper, 25.7 × 17.1
Bequeathed by Gabrielle Keiller 1995
GMA 3987

Wilhelm Lehmbruck 1881–1919 · Head of a Girl Looking over her Shoulder (Mädchenkopf, sich umwendend) 1913–14

Terracotta,
39.5 × 27 × 18.5
Purchased 1993
GMA 3731

Born in Duisburg (where there is now a Lehmbruck Museum), Lehmbruck studied in Düsseldorf. His early work was influenced by Rodin and the Belgian sculptor Constantin Meunier, but his mature work owes more to Maillol. In this Head we can sense the concern with calm, classical values that are exemplified in Maillol's Eve (see p.22). Lehmbruck lived in Paris from 1911 until 1914 when, owing to the outbreak of war, he had to return to Germany. He worked in a military hospital and during the latter stages of

the war suffered bouts of severe depression. He committed suicide in 1919, aged just thirty-eight.

This Head derives from a life-size sculpture of a limbless female figure looking over her left shoulder. Adopting a practice popularised by Rodin, Lehmbruck made several variants of the component parts, casting the head alone in terracotta, bronze and cement. This cast is probably posthumous, and may have been made by the Lehmbruck family in the 1930s.

Ernst Barlach 1870–1938 · *The Terrible Year 1937 (Das Schlimme Jahr 1937)* 1936

Barlach studied sculpture in Dresden. He made his first wooden sculptures in 1907 and, in common with a number of German sculptors, wood remained his preferred medium. However, Barlach stands slightly apart from some of the German Expressionist sculptors in that he was not attracted to abstraction and rarely distorted the human body beyond simplifying it. His inspiration came more from North German Gothic art and, typically, he presents the human figure in a state of suffering and misery.

Barlach was an outspoken opponent of the Nazi party, and as a result his works began to disappear from museum displays in the mid-1930s. Although carved in 1936, *The Terrible Year 1937* was given its allegorical title the following year in response to Hitler's notorious Degenerate 'Art' exhibition, in which Barlach and a host of contemporary artists were included. By the summer of 1937, nearly 400 of Barlach's works had been confiscated from German museums. This rare and poignant survival is the only wood carving by Barlach in a public collection in Britain.

Oak, 142 × 31 × 28.5
Purchased with assistance from the National Art Collections Fund (William Leng Bequest) 1987
GMA 3036

Otto Dix 1891–1969 · Nude Girl on a Fur (Mädchen auf Fell) 1932

*Tempera and oil on canvas
laid on wood,
98.5 × 142.8
Purchased 1980*
GMA 2195

Dix was one of the leading artists of the German *Neue Sachlichkeit* (New Objectivity) school. After the war he began a series of satirical paintings depicting war cripples and prostitutes: some were so shocking they were banned from exhibition. For several years he had painted in a style which fused Expressionism with Futurism, but by the early 1920s he had adopted a very detailed, realist style, and a technique based on the Old Masters. He would cover the canvas or wood with a layer of gesso, paint with egg tempera, and then apply thin glazes which allowed the underlying colours to glow through.

The Old Masters also inspired his compositions even though his themes were mainly contemporary. The pose of *Nude Girl on a Fur* relates to the work of German Renaissance artists such as Cranach and Dürer. Compared to his preliminary sketch the pose in the finished painting is ungainly, unnatural even, the girl's left leg having been twisted towards the viewer so that her sex is displayed at the very centre of the composition. Dix was always prepared to alter what he saw in order to heighten the sense of unglamourised reality. This attitude was not appreciated by Hitler's National Socialist party though, for when they came to power in 1933, Dix was dismissed from his teaching post at the Dresden Academy.

Oskar Kokoschka 1886–1980 · *Zrání (Summer)* 1938/40

Invalided out of the army during the First World War, Kokoschka was based mainly in Dresden until 1923. He spent the years from 1924 to 1930 travelling and from 1931 to 1934 returned to live in his native Vienna. In 1934 he moved to Prague, where he took out Czech citizenship. After the Munich Agreement of September 1938, which effectively delivered Czechoslovakia into the hands of the Nazis, he flew to London with his future wife, Olda Palkovská. He was able to take just one painting with him, *Girls Bathing*, which he had to pawn; he managed to buy it back shortly afterwards. The painting was exhibited early in 1939 and a contemporary photograph of it shows a nude bather in the foreground, her arms spread wide, and another bather, viewed from behind, in the distance. Some time afterwards, probably late in 1940, Kokoschka reworked the entire painting, leaving almost none of the original composition untouched. The landscape probably combines elements from the Cornish coast around Polperro, where the artist lived for nearly a year in 1939–40, with memories of the Bohemian country-side. The painting offers an idyllic vision of leisure and contentment, in stark contrast to the turmoil upsetting central Europe at that time. The Czech title *Zrání* has no precise English translation but approximates to 'maturity', 'ripening' and 'summer'.

The painting was given to the National Gallery of Scotland on behalf of the Czechoslovak Government in Exile in 1942. The Gallery's rule that the work of living artists could not be acquired was waived on this occasion.

Oil on canvas, 68.3 × 89.2
Presented by the Czechoslo-vak Government in Exile 1942
GMA 21

Francis Picabia 1879–1953 · Girl Born without a Mother (Fille née sans mère) c.1916–17

Gouache and metallic paint
on printed paper, 50 × 65
Purchased 1990
GMA 3545

Picabia's work shifted from Impressionism to Fauvism and from Cubism to abstraction, then took its own rather bizarre course. Like his friend Marcel Duchamp (see pp.66–67), Picabia moved to New York in 1915, becoming a central figure in the newly emerging proto-Dada groups. That year he embarked upon a series of drawings which are full of mordant satire, using the machine as an ironic metaphor for human life and suggesting that life is essentially a nihilistic enterprise sustained by basic mechanical instincts. Picabia stated that his visit to America had brought about this revolution in his work: 'The machine has become more than a mere adjunct to life. It is really part of human life – perhaps the very soul. In

seeking forms through which to interpret ideas or by which to expose human characteristics I have come at length upon the form which appears most brilliantly plastic and fraught with symbolism.'

This work was made in Barcelona, where Picabia lived from July 1916 to spring 1917. It was painted over a fold-out illustration of a stationary steam engine, probably found in a technical journal relating to railway engineering. In painting over the diagram Picabia erased some elements and added others. By virtue of its title, the painting alludes, mockingly, to the creation of Eve from Adam's rib and also to the Virgin birth (the gold background may refer to early Renaissance paintings of the Virgin and Child).

Man Ray 1890–1976

These are rare and important works dating from the early stages of New York Dada. During the First World War, Picabia and Duchamp (see opposite and pp.66–67) fled France for New York, where they came to the attention of young American artists such as Man Ray, who was from Philadelphia. Inspired by them, Man Ray began making paintings, collages and photographs of a mechanistic, Dada nature. For Dada artists, the collage was a means of de-personalising art, of negating the humanist values associated with traditional easel painting. Speaking of his work of this period Man Ray said that 'The new subjects were of pseudo-mechanistic forms, more or less invented, but suggesting geometric contraptions that were neither logical nor scientific.' The word 'involute' means intricate and curled: this collage invokes the term both literally and metaphorically. It is composed of involuted, spiralling forms; and the letters 'INV' coupled with the 'O' beneath and the cut-out metal lute spell out the title in a visual pun. The long screw form on the left is echoed by the actual screw which holds the metal plate in place; the threads in a transparent wallet, tacked on to the picture, refer to the strings of the lute.

Aviary depicts the artist's New York studio, complete with the dressmaker's dummy Man Ray said he kept for company. Once more, the technique – airbrush – was designed to counter traditional fine art practices. The French title, *La Volière*, is slang for a brothel.

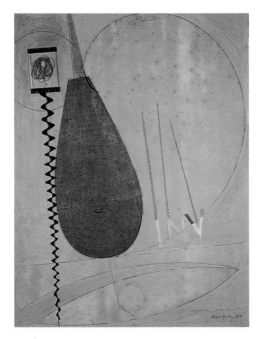

Involute 1917
Mixed-media collage on card laid on board,
61.5 × 46.5
Purchased 1978
GMA 2064

Aviary (La Volière) 1919
Airbrushed ink, pen and ink and pencil on card, 70 × 55
Purchased with assistance from the Heritage Lottery Fund and the National Art Collections Fund 1995
GMA 3888

Leather-covered case
containing miniature
replicas and photographs of
Duchamp's works,
10 × 38 × 40.5 (closed)
Presented by Gabrielle
Keiller 1989
GMA 3472

Duchamp was intrigued by the idea that ordinary, mass-produced things could be considered as art objects in their own right. He virtually stopped painting after 1912, preferring simply to sign, and sometimes alter, household objects. He called these works 'Readymades'. Eventually, anything he signed came to be considered an 'original Duchamp'. His questioning attitude towards definitions of authenticity, originality, artistry and authorship has been immensely influential.

This leather case contains sixty-nine painstakingly accurate reproductions of works made by Duchamp throughout his career. Twenty-two de-luxe versions of the case were made, each featuring a different hand-coloured 'original' fixed to the inside of the lid. Three hundred standard versions in a cardboard case were also envisaged. Ours is number two of the de-luxe edition. For Duchamp there was no clear distinction between the original and the reproduction, a concept cleverly embodied in Box in a Suitcase. He stated: 'Instead of painting something new, my aim was to reproduce the paintings and the objects I liked and collect them in a space as small as possible ... Then it occurred to me that it could be a box in which all my works would be collected and mounted like in a small museum, a portable museum, so to speak.'

Marcel Duchamp 1887–1968

Between 1950 and 1954 Duchamp made four small-scale erotic objects, casts of two of which belong to the Gallery. Their form is deliberately enigmatic and suggestive. *Female Fig-leaf* was made in 1950 and was originally cast in plaster. Duchamp gave one of the two plasters as a parting gift to his friend Man Ray, who left New York for Paris in 1951. Ten bronze casts were made in 1961. The original version of *Wedge of Chastity* was made in 1954 in plaster and dental plastic, making the work look like a tooth set in the gum. Eight bronze casts were made in 1963: our cast was made especially for Duchamp.

Duchamp did not divulge the manufacturing process of either work, but *Female Fig-leaf* may be an actual cast of a woman's genitals. *Wedge of Chastity* has similarly erotic connotations, there being 'male' and 'female' parts which fit snugly together. He originally made *Wedge of Chastity* as a gift for his wife Teeny. Duchamp later explained: 'It was my wedding present to her ... We usually take it with us, like a wedding ring.'

Female Fig-leaf (Feuille de vigne femelle) 1950/61
Bronze, 9 × 14 × 12.5
Bequeathed by Gabrielle Keiller 1995
GMA 3967

Wedge of Chastity (Coin de chasteté) 1954/63
Bronze and dental plastic, 5.7 × 8.5 × 4.2
Bequeathed by Gabrielle Keiller 1995
GMA 3968

Max Ernst 1891–1976

*Max Ernst Showing a
Young Girl the Head of
his Father (Max Ernst
montrant à une jeune
fille la tête de son père)*
c.1926–27
Oil on canvas,
114.3 × 146.8
Accepted by H.M.
Government in lieu of
Inheritance Tax
(Gabrielle Keiller Collection)
and allocated to the Scottish
National Gallery of Modern
Art 1998
GMA 3972

The Gallery has an outstanding
collection of Max Ernst's work,
including eleven paintings and
collages ranging in date from about
1914 to 1937, as well as a number of
drawings and prints. Ernst was born
near Cologne in Germany. After the
war he became the leader of the
Cologne Dada group. He stated that
'Dada was a rebellious upsurge of vital
energy and rage; it resulted from the
absurdity, the whole immense
stupidity of that imbecilic war. We
young people came back from the war
in a state of stupefaction, and our rage
had to find expression somehow or
other. This it did quite naturally
through attacks on the foundations of
the civilisation responsible for war.'
Hat in Hand, Hat on Head stands at the
beginning of Ernst's Dada period. The
disembodied, moustached man doffs
his bowler hat, only to reveal another
underneath (the mark of the true
bourgeois gentleman).

In 1919 Ernst began using collage –
a technique which challenged the
traditional supremacy of oil paint.
Katharina Ondulata is one of his most
famous collages. Made while he was
still living in Cologne, the work is
infused with the Dada spirit of whimsy
and anarchy, but it anticipates themes
which would interest the Surrealists
(cosmic imagery, the battle of the
sexes). The full title of the work,
written along its bottom margin,
translates as 'Undulating Katharina,
i.e. mistress of the inn on the Lahn
appears as guardian angel and

mother-of-pearl of the Germans on cork soles in the zodiac sign of cancer.' The 'mistress of the inn' would appear to be represented by the revolving sun on the left which also doubles as a Catherine wheel. The male is represented by a stick-like mannequin: his fuse is alight, ready to trigger his sexual desires.

Ernst moved to Paris in 1922 and became a central figure in the Surrealist group. His Oedipal conflicts with his father seem to be highlighted in the large and majestic *Max Ernst Showing a Young Girl the Head of his Father*. The 'young girl' may be Ernst's dead sister, in which case an incestuous triangle of father, son and daughter is implied. Ernst was a pioneer of accidental effects in painting and drawing. Here, the forest (a favourite subject of German Romantic artists) is executed via a technique known as *grattage*, whereby the painted canvas is laid over a rough wooden surface and scraped to produce a rich, grainy texture.

Hat in Hand, Hat on Head (Hut in der Hand, Hut auf dem Kopf) c.1919
Oil on board, 36.8 × 29.2
Purchased with assistance from the National Art Collections Fund 1997
GMA 4169

Katharina Ondulata 1920
Gouache, pencil and ink on printed paper,
31.5 × 27.5
Purchased with assistance from the Heritage Lottery Fund and the National Art Collections Fund 1995
GMA 3885

Joan Miró 1893–1983

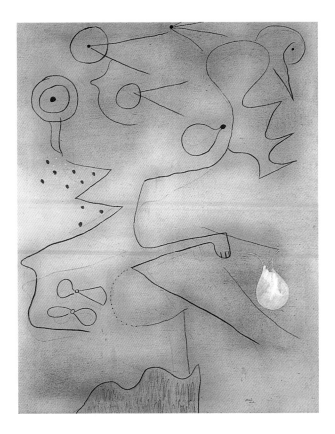

Painting (Peinture)
1925
Oil and black chalk on
canvas, 140 × 113.5
Purchased 1979
GMA 2078

Miró was born in Barcelona and
moved to Paris in 1920. His early
work combined miniaturist detail
with a Cubist fragmentation of space.
In Paris he abandoned this style and
began to paint an imaginary world
full of strange, insect-like figures and
forms which seem to float in space.
This fantastic sign language, which
was partly inspired by dreams, soon
became a hallmark of Surrealist art.
Maternity, an early Surrealist masterpiece, was probably painted in the
summer or autumn of 1924 at
Montroig, near Barcelona, where
Miró's parents had a country home.
In August Miró wrote to a friend
saying that 'My latest canvases are
conceived like a bolt from the blue,
absolutely detached from the outer
world (the world of men who have

two eyes in the space below the
forehead).' *Maternity* has its origins in
a postcard of a Spanish dancer but the
only vestige left in the painting is the
pierced skirt, which apes the dancer's
polka-dot dress. Two insect-like
infants, one male, the other female,
are suspended from their mother's
breasts.

André Breton's *First Surrealist
Manifesto*, published in October 1924,
defined Surrealism as 'Pure psychic
automatism, by which one intends to
express verbally, in writing or by other
method, the real functioning of the
mind. Dictation by thought, in the
absence of any control exercised by
reason, and beyond any aesthetic or
moral preoccupation.' Breton's ideas
(see p.84) were indebted to Sigmund
Freud, who argued that subconscious
urges underlie our everyday thoughts
and actions. The Surrealists believed
that the subconscious should be
made to speak for itself. One way of
doing this, they said, was through
'automatic' drawing, that is, drawing
or painting in an unpremeditated
manner. It was argued that the results
would reveal hidden truths normally
locked away in the subconscious.
Miró was the most celebrated
exponent of 'automatic painting' and
for this reason Breton called him 'the
most Surrealist of us all'. Ironically,
though, Miró never joined the
Surrealist group because he objected
to dogma and officialdom. Legend
has it that he would sometimes paint
in a state of hallucination owing to
extreme hunger. However, these so-
called automatic paintings are not as
random as they may at first seem, for
many of them are preceded by
sketches. No sketch survives for
Painting, but the preliminary chalk
underdrawing is still clearly visible.

Maternity (Maternité) 1924
Oil on canvas, 92.1 × 73.1
Purchased with assistance from the National Heritage Memorial Fund, the
National Art Collections Fund (William Leng Fund) and public donations 1991
GMA 3589

Yves Tanguy 1900–55

they seem to reappear, as if in dream-like scenes, in his paintings. His background in the merchant navy (his father and grandfather were also seamen) may also be relevant, for the paintings suggest subaquatic land-scapes. It is an elemental, half gassy, half liquid world, giving rise to primitive, amoeba-like forms. The theme of genesis and the birth of the world was popular with the Surreal-ists, particularly Miró, whose work seems to have had a strong impact upon Tanguy; and the idea of meta-morphosis, of one shape changing into another, is also central to Surrealism. *Outside* is one of the largest and most impressive of Tanguy's early paintings. He was the most untheoretical of artists and preferred not to explain or discuss his work; indeed he said that it could not and should not be explained. Like dreams, they resisted logical explanation.

The Ribbon of Excess is an important work in Tanguy's oeuvre, marking a

Outside (Dehors) 1929
Oil on canvas, 116 × 89.5
Purchased with assistance
from the Heritage Lottery
Fund and the National Art
Collections Fund 1995
GMA 3893

Tanguy's decision to become an artist is part of Surrealist mythology. In 1923, while riding on a bus, he caught sight of two paintings by Giorgio de Chirico in the window of a Paris art gallery and decided there and then to become a painter. He had no formal art education or arts background: he had previously been in the merchant navy, worked in a press agency, and done various other odd jobs. By 1925 he had met André Breton and joined the Surrealist group.

Tanguy's family came from the Finistère area of Brittany and as a child he spent his summer holidays there. The prehistoric menhirs and dolmens left a strong impression on him, and

Never Again (Plus Jamais) 1939
Oil on canvas, 92 × 73
Bequeathed by Gabrielle Keiller 1995
GMA 4085

shift from the spacious 'underwater landscapes' of the late 1920s to a world packed with intricately-drawn, bean-like forms. These works of the 1930s, in which the weird objects cast long, hard shadows, suggest desert or Martian landscapes as much as subaquatic worlds. The strange geological features Tanguy saw on a trip to Africa in 1930 may have influenced this change in direction, and his friendship with sculptors such as Giacometti and Arp (see pp.76–77 and 83) may also be relevant. *Never Again* was painted shortly before Tanguy left France for New York in November 1939. Thereafter he remained in the USA, becoming an American citizen in 1948.

Outside and *The Ribbon of Excess* both belonged to the poet Paul Eluard, who was a close friend of the artist. By different routes they subsequently passed into the collection of Roland Penrose, the English artist and authority on Surrealism (see p.124).

The Ribbon of Excess
(Le Ruban des excès) 1932
Oil on wood, 35 × 45.2
Accepted by H.M. Government in lieu of
Inheritance Tax (Gabrielle Keiller Collection) and
allocated to the Scottish National Gallery of
Modern Art 1998
GMA 4084

Salvador Dalí 1904–89 · Bird (Oiseau) 1928

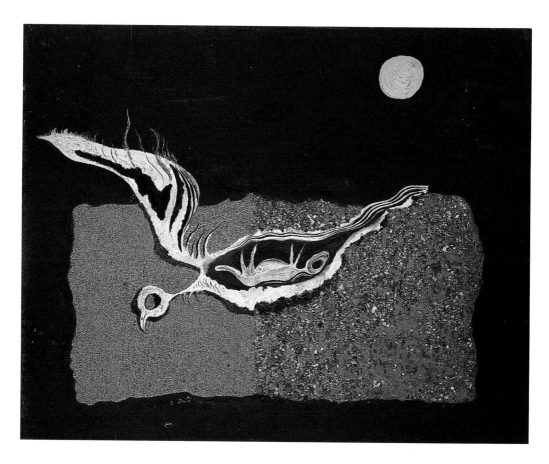

Oil, sand and shingle on board, 49.7 × 61
Purchased with assistance from the Heritage Lottery Fund and the National Art Collections Fund 1995
GMA 3883

Dalí was thrown out of art school in Madrid in 1923, and in the next few years ran through a gamut of styles, quickly establishing himself as one of the most notorious young Catalan painters. By 1927 he was moving away from Cubism into a Surrealist style which owed much to the recent work of Tanguy and Miró. Though based in Spain, Dalí was keenly aware of recent developments in Surrealist art and literature in Paris. He met Miró, a fellow Catalan, in 1927, but only met other members of the Surrealist group when he visited Paris in 1929. He joined the group towards the end of that year.

Bird was painted in Cadaqués, a fishing village where the Dalí family had a summer house. Many of Dalí's works of this period depict beach scenes, and Bird literally incorporates the beach: the portion on the left is made up of sand, while the patch on the right is coarser shingle. Rotting animals are represented in a number of Dalí's works of this period. However, the exact subject of this painting seems to be indebted to André Breton. In his book Clair de Terre of 1923, Breton recounts a dream in which he and some friends were swimming in the sea when they startled two birds. One of the group shot at the birds as they flew overhead. By the time they had been washed ashore the birds had changed into creatures resembling a cow or horse.

Salvador Dalí 1904–89 · The Signal of Anguish (Le Signal de l'angoisse) c.1932–36

Dalí constructed his public profile and his paintings with equal care and attention. Despite his non-conformist behaviour, he was a great admirer of the Old Masters and was a supremely gifted technician. The combination of flamboyant character and meticulous craftsmanship made him a celebrity by the age of thirty, when he had his first exhibition in New York.

This painting probably has its origins in an article Dalí wrote in 1931. In the text – like many of Dalí's paintings and writings it concerns masturbatory fantasies – he refers to a hidden voyeur who watches the object of his desire through the window of a dilapidated building. Though this painting is dated 1936, it was reproduced in a magazine in 1934 and may even have been painted a year or two earlier. Minor alterations were made in 1936, namely the addition of a leafy branch which crosses the woman's shoulder, and slight changes to the cypress tree in the background. The painting is typical of Dalí's works of the early 1930s in which there is a shift from the clear blue skies of his earlier work to landscapes bathed in a golden, autumnal glow.

Oil on wood, 21.8 × 16.2
Bequeathed by Gabrielle Keiller 1995
GMA 3956

Alberto Giacometti 1901–66 · Disagreeable Object, to be Disposed of (Objet désagréable, à jeter) 1931

Wood, 19.6 × 31 × 29
Purchased 1990
GMA 3547

In 1922 Giacometti moved from his native Switzerland to Paris, where he studied under Bourdelle (see p.23). He experimented with Cubism for a brief period but by 1930 was making strange objects suggestive of cruelty, danger, sex and dreams; that year he joined the Surrealist group.

Disagreeable Object, to be Disposed of has two horns on one side, one on the other. It is meant to be picked up and played with and can stand in several different positions. It is at once funny but sinister, offensive yet satisfying to hold and handle. Crafted with deliberation and precision, it seems built for a purpose, though the nature of that purpose (something sexual seems likely) can only be guessed at. Giacometti made just a few wooden

sculptures of this kind in the early 1930s. It is similar to a type of low stool made in western Africa, though here one of the 'legs' is fixed incongruously to the top of the 'seat'.

The French title of the work is slightly ambiguous and may also be translated as Disagreeable Object, to be Thrown Away, or Thrown. It has also been known as Sculpture without Base and Object without Base.

Alberto Giacometti 1901–66 · *Woman with her Throat Cut (Femme égorgée)* 1932

Woman with her Throat Cut is the most complex and macabre of all Giacometti's Surrealist sculptures. It suggests a variety of conflicting states: pain and ecstasy, human and insect, attractive and repulsive. Although the woman appears to be in the throes of death, her taut, aggressive form also looks like a trap – a fly-eating plant or a man trap, primed to shut tight were the body to be touched. The right leg folds under the abdomen to form a spiked rib-cage. The throat, rendered as an exposed wind-pipe with a little nick in it, evokes the dying figure's last desperate gasps for breath. One hand is represented as a kind of shovel while the other is a cigar-shaped pod which can swivel around on a limited axis. Giacometti said that this element referred to the nightmare of not being able to lift one's hand against an attacker, as if the woman had been unable to defend herself. The specta-tor is thus drawn into the gruesome murder, invited to swing the pod and touch an object which looks as if it might suddenly spring to life and turn predator. The resemblance to scorpi-ons and praying mantises may be pertinent since in both cases the female sometimes devours the male after mating. The sculpture may also have been inspired by a short story about the serial killer Jack the Ripper, written by one of the artist's friends. While such subjects are popular in novels and films, they are often considered taboo in painting and sculpture – which is perhaps why Giacometti chose them.

Bronze, 22 × 87.5 × 53.5
Purchased 1970
GMA 1109

René Magritte 1898–1967

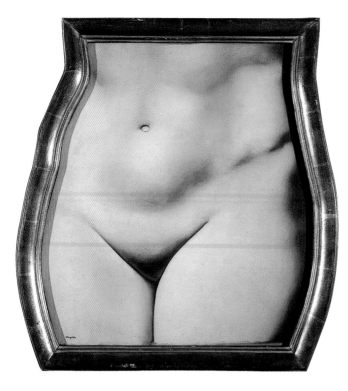

Representation
(La Représentation)
1937
Oil on canvas laid on
plywood, 48.8 × 44.5
Purchased 1990
GMA 3546

The Gallery owns four exceptional paintings by René Magritte. Magritte was born in Belgium and apart from a few years spent in the Paris suburbs in the late 1920s, lived there all his life. In the 1920s and 1930s Brussels was second only to Paris as a centre of Surrealist activity.

Unlike Ernst and Miró, Magritte did not subscribe to the view that the unconscious could be expressed through chance or 'automatic' techniques; instead, he planned and executed his paintings with all the deliberation and *trompe-l'oeil* skill of an academic painter. The results are surprisingly credible images of seemingly illogical scenes. Magritte's deadpan style owed much to Giorgio de Chirico, and like de Chirico, Magritte would undermine the logic of illusionism by tampering with scale and by placing unrelated objects in

unexpected settings. A constant theme running through Magritte's art is the equivocal relationship that exists between the painted image and the visible world, between what we think of as fiction and reality. Magritte's art blurs the boundaries between the two.

The Magic Mirror was painted in 1929 during Magritte's three-year period of residence near Paris. It is one of a series of 'word paintings' made in the late 1920s in which the words and the image seem to conflict with each other. Even the identity of the object is uncertain, despite the clarity of presentation. *Threatening Weather* was painted during the summer of the same year while Magritte was staying with Dalí near Cadaqués, in Spain. Painted early in 1937, *Representation* was originally square in format though by May of that year the artist had cut it down, mounted it on plywood, and had a new frame specially made. It is the only shaped frame in Magritte's oeuvre. Dalí had deployed shaped frames around a pair of 'portraits' painted a year earlier, and Magritte may have seen these when he visited the collector Edward James in London in February 1937. Shortly after finishing the work Magritte wrote to André Breton, telling him he had done 'the framed section of a female body ... It constitutes a rather surprising object, I think.'

Probably painted in the second half of 1937, *The Black Flag* may refer to the German bombing of the small Spanish town of Guernica in April 1937. Magritte later stated in a letter to Breton that the picture 'gave a foretaste of the terror which would come from flying machines, and I am not proud of it.' In contrast to Léger (see p.33) Magritte was showing that machines have their darker side.

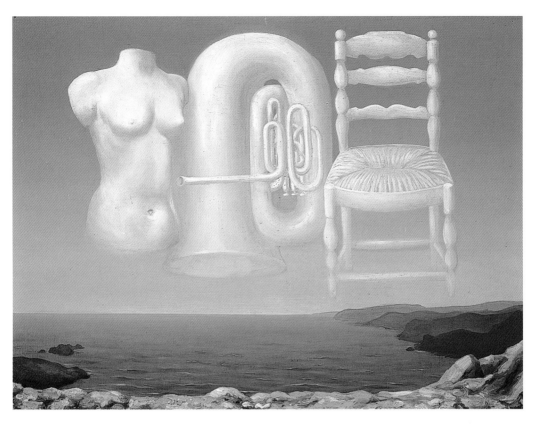

Threatening Weather (Le Temps menaçant) 1929
Oil on canvas, 54 × 73. Purchased with assistance from the Heritage Lottery Fund
and the National Art Collections Fund 1995
GMA 3887

The Black Flag (Le Drapeau noir) 1937
Oil on canvas, 54.2 × 73.7. Purchased 1972
GMA 1261

The Magic Mirror
(Le Miroir magique) 1929
Oil on canvas, 73 × 54.5
Bequeathed by Gabrielle Keiller 1995
GMA 3997

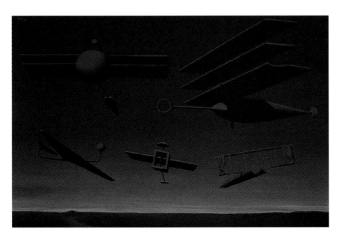

Paul Delvaux 1897–1994

Next to Magritte (see pp.78–79), Delvaux was the leading Belgian artist associated with Surrealism. However, he was never a member of the Surrealist group and, living in Belgium, he had little contact with the main figures in the movement. Like Magritte and Tanguy, Delvaux was strongly influenced by de Chirico's work, which he saw in an exhibition of Surrealist art held in Brussels in 1934. Within two years his art had changed from a quirky Expressionist style to one of dream landscapes populated by mysterious female nudes. Call of the Night and Street of the Trams are early and important works in this style, the first completed in March 1938, the second in January 1939.

From the late 1930s until his death in 1994 at the age of ninety-six, Delvaux's art changed little. The female figures all look much alike and the same poses reappear in different paintings – indeed the figures in these two paintings are similar. The backgrounds often feature classical architecture or Brussels buildings (Delvaux had initially trained as an architect). Trams (in Freud's terms classic sexual metaphors) are a recurrent theme. Male figures seldom appear, and when they do it is usually in the form of a bespectacled, frock-coated professor, intent on some scholarly purpose and apparently oblivious to the amply endowed nudes who stand idly by. There is a deliberate mismatch between the eroticism of the nudes and the uninviting settings into which they have been cast. Sexual fantasy collides with sexual anxiety. In Call of the Night we find a desolate landscape, littered with a skull and skeleton, while rampant vegetation clings to the languid nudes. The symbolism calls for interpretation but resists any.

Street of the Trams
(La Rue du tramway) 1938–39
Oil on canvas, 90.3 × 130.5
Bequeathed by Gabrielle Keiller 1995
GMA 3692

Call of the Night
(L'Appel de la nuit) 1938
Oil on canvas, 110 × 145
Purchased with assistance from the Heritage Lottery Fund and the National Art Collections Fund 1995
GMA 3884

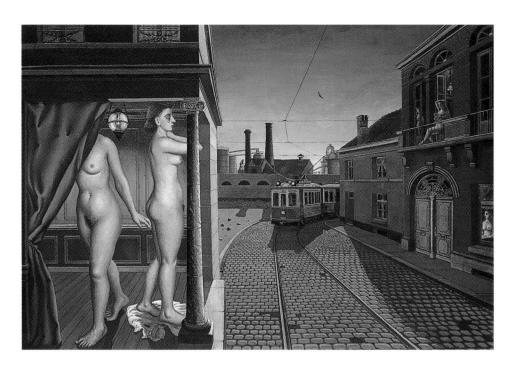

Alexander Calder 1898–1976 · *Spider* c.1935–37

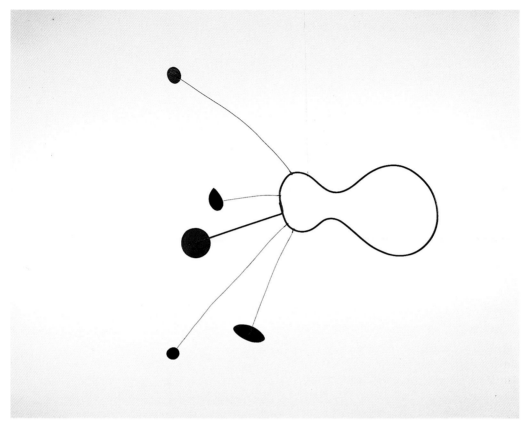

Metal, painted,
104 × 89 × 0.7
Purchased 1976
GMA 1586

The son of a successful sculptor, Calder was American but made frequent trips to Paris where he was friendly with the Surrealists. In the mid-1920s he made a number of small wire figures and animals which eventually formed a complete miniature circus.

He began making abstract sculptures in 1930, following a visit to Mondrian's studio. Some of his early works incorporated motors while others moved of their own accord; Calder christened the latter works 'mobiles', a term suggested to him by Marcel Duchamp. Since he had trained as an engineer Calder was well acquainted with the mechanical principles required to make the works balance and move freely.

Spider is among the earliest of these hanging mobiles which, with their poetic, floating forms, look like three-dimensional equivalents of Miró's paintings. It has been suggested that they have a source in scientific models of the planetary system.

Jean Arp 1886–1966 · Rising up (S'élevant) 1962

Arp was born in Strasbourg, a German city until it was ceded to France in the peace treaty following the First World War. Christened Hans, he later adopted the French form of the name, Jean.

Arp lived in Switzerland during the war, becoming a founder-member of the Zurich Dada group. During this period and in the 1920s he made wooden reliefs, collages and drawings. He moved to France in 1925 and only began to make free-standing sculpture in the 1930s, producing strange, vegetable forms he called 'human concretions' – a term chosen to suggest that they might have grown out of the human body. Arp continued to work in this way through to the 1960s. He did not consider these works as abstract, but rather as organic forms which had occurred naturally: 'Art is a fruit that grows in man, like a fruit on a plant, or a child in its mother's womb. But whereas the fruit of the plant, the fruit of the mother's womb, assume autonomous and natural forms, art, the spiritual fruit of man, usually shows an absurd resemblance to the aspect of something else.'

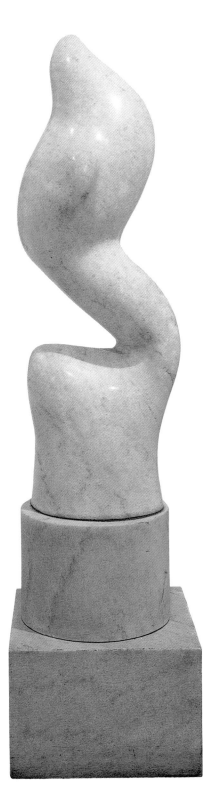

Marble,
176.5 × 44.5 × 44.5
Purchased 1970
GMA 1253

André Breton 1896–1966 · *Poem-Object (Poème-Objet)* 1935

Mixed media on wood,
16.3 × 20.7
Purchased 1993
GMA 3737

André Breton was the organising hand behind the Surrealist movement. He served as a medical auxiliary during the First World War and soon discovered the writings of Freud, Charcot and Janet. Their books dwelt upon issues of psychiatry, the unconscious and insanity – issues which would appeal greatly to the Surrealists. In 1920 Breton abandoned his medical studies in order to concentrate on literary and artistic matters.

By 1924 he had become a prominent figure in the Parisian avant-garde and had gathered around him a group of poets and artists interested in exploring the subconscious. In October he launched the Surrealist movement with his *Manifesto of Surrealism* and thereafter he became the mastermind of the new group, attracting prospective members and expelling those whose views contradicted his own.

A number of Surrealist artists, including Miró, Giacometti and Dalí, began making strange object-sculptures in the early 1930s. Although Breton was known primarily as a poet, critic and strategist, he made about a dozen of his own assemblages in the 1930s and early 1940s, calling them 'Poem-Objects'. The text on the plaster egg in this work translates as 'I see / I imagine' and the poem beneath consists of the following, deliberately cryptic lines: 'At the intersection of the invisible lines of force / Find / The point of the song towards which the trees help themselves rise up / The thorn of silence / which wants the master of the ships to give the wind his / plume of blue dogs.'

Joseph Cornell 1903–72 · Untitled (Bird Box) c.1948

Cornell never went to art school, never travelled to Europe and led a quiet life at the family home in Flushing, New York State. In 1931 he saw an exhibition of Max Ernst's collages at the Julien Levy gallery in New York and he soon began making his own collages and small assemblages; he exhibited at Levy's gallery the following year. By the mid-1930s Cornell was making shadow-box constructions, filling them with the bits and pieces he found on his regular visits to New York bookshops and junkshops: mirrors, maps, postcards, glasses, dolls, marbles, balls, stamps and the like. These carefully crafted assemblages develop from the Dada and Surrealist constructions of artists like Schwitters, Duchamp and Breton (see pp. 58, 66–67 and opposite), though by the mid-1930s many of the Surrealists were making such 'object sculptures'. Although Cornell often took part in exhibitions of Surrealist art, he was on the fringes of the movement. While many of the Surrealists were interested in the subconscious and shocking imagery for its own sake, Cornell's art was more personal and idiosyncratic. With its constant references to the past in the form of toys, collecting and old scrap-book images, his work conjures up an enigmatic, slightly sinister vision of childhood.

Mixed media in glass-fronted wooden box with electric light,
32 × 23.3 × 11.2
Bequeathed by Gabrielle Keiller 1995
GMA 3950

Wood, painted,
122 × 46 × 46
Purchased 1989
GMA 3447

Mackintosh was born and raised in Glasgow. He became an architect (his greatest achievement is Glasgow School of Art) but was also intimately concerned with aspects of interior design, including the design of furniture, wallpaper, fabrics and cutlery.

This revolving bookcase was made for Hous'hill, a large nineteenth-century house belonging to Catherine Cranston and her husband Major Cochrane, at Nitshill in Glasgow. Miss Cranston had earlier commissioned Mackintosh to design a series of tea rooms in Glasgow, including the famous Willow Tea Rooms which opened in 1904. In 1903 she asked him to redecorate some of the rooms at Hous'hill and also design new furniture. This, Mackintosh's only revolving bookcase, was destined for the drawing room. The design is based on an organic principle, with the vertical divisions representing the boughs and branches of a tree which multiply at each shelf, ending in little painted squares which suggest blossom or leaves. Mackintosh's geometric but organic furniture had a powerful influence on turn-of-the-century architecture and design in Europe, particularly in Vienna.

Besides being an architect and designer, Mackintosh also produced a large number of drawings and watercolours. Many of his earliest works are pencil sketches of buildings, and later on he produced a series of delicate watercolours of plants. Following the collapse of his architectural practice, in 1923 he and his wife, Margaret Macdonald, moved to the south of France, staying for most of the time at a hotel in Port Vendres, a small town close to the Spanish border. (Collioure, where Derain had painted, and Banyuls-sur-Mer, where Maillol lived, were just a couple of miles away: see pp.20 and 22.) *Mont Alba* is one of about forty surviving landscape watercolours that Mackintosh painted in the area during their stay. These watercolours have the same sense of organic structure that we find in Mackintosh's architecture. Owing to ill health he returned to London in 1927; he died there the following year.

Watercolour on paper,
38.7 × 43.8
Purchased 1990
GMA 3533

William Orpen 1878–1931 · A Bloomsbury Family 1907

Oil on canvas, 86.5 × 91.5
Presented by the Scottish
Modern Arts Association
1964
GMA 881

Orpen moved from his native Dublin to London in 1897, becoming one of the most successful society portraitists of his day. *A Bloomsbury Family* depicts Orpen's friend, the artist William Nicholson, with his family at their home in Mecklenburgh Square, Bloomsbury. Nicholson's wife, the painter Mabel Pryde (sister of James Pryde: see opposite), is standing by the door. In a preliminary sketch for the painting she featured more promi-nently in the foreground, standing protectively over the child, and X-ray photographs show that the painting originally followed that scheme. Sitting at the table from left to right are the Nicholson children: Nancy, who married the writer Robert Graves; Tony, who died during the war in 1918; and Ben, who would become Britain's foremost abstract artist (see pp.110

and 122). Standing in the foreground is Christopher or 'Kit', wearing a type of frock often worn by young boys at this date. He became an architect. Orpen himself is reflected in the convex mirror.

The Nicholsons lived in Bloomsbury only from 1906 to 1907, and were not part of the Bloomsbury Group (see p.98). William Nicholson was peeved by the title Orpen gave the painting when it was first exhibited in 1908, since by then the family had moved to the more stylish district of Chelsea: he thought Bloomsbury dull and unfashionable by comparison.

James Pryde 1866–1941 · Lumber: A Silhouette c.1921

Pryde was born in Edinburgh. He grew up with a love of the theatre and even worked for a time (without much success) as an actor; later in life he designed theatre sets. Living in London from 1890, Pryde and his brother-in-law William Nicholson (portrayed in Orpen's *A Bloomsbury Family*: see opposite) set up partnership as poster artists under the name 'The Beggarstaff Brothers'. Their modern, simplified style would revolutionise poster design.

In about 1909 Pryde began a series of paintings called *The Human Comedy*, which were loosely based on his recollection of a seventeenth-century four-poster bed at the palace of Holyroodhouse in Edinburgh. The bed was said to have been slept in by Mary, Queen of Scots. Pryde conceived a series of twelve works, but had a thirteenth in progress at the time of his death. These curious, sombre paintings, feature an enormous bed, very much taller than the original at Holyrood, looming over the small figures who act out various narratives. The subjects include a doctor visiting a patient, a convalescent and a death scene. In *Lumber: A Silhouette*, a brooding figure stands beside the tattered bed, with odd bits of furniture – the 'lumber' indicated in the title – scattered about. The exaggerations of scale, melodramatic lighting effects and even the broad, painterly technique, owe much to Pryde's interest in the theatre.

Oil on canvas,
151.8 × 131.1
Purchased 1975
GMA 1521

Samuel John Peploe 1871–1935 · The Black Bottle c.1905

Oil on canvas, 50.8 × 61
Presented by Mr J. W. Blyth
1939
GMA 26

Peploe is one of the group of four artists collectively known as the 'Scottish Colourists'; the others are Cadell, Hunter and Fergusson (see opposite and the following pages). Although now in common usage and giving the impression that the four constituted a coherent group, the term 'Scottish Colourists' seems to have been first employed only in 1948, when three of the four artists were already dead. Peploe and Fergusson were good friends, as were Peploe and Cadell, and all four exhibited at one time or another with the same Glasgow dealer, but their differences are as evident as their similarities. What they really shared was their love of brilliant colour, acquired largely through their knowledge of recent French painting.

Peploe was born in Edinburgh and studied in Paris. As *The Black Bottle* indicates, Peploe was not immediately drawn to the blond tonalities of French Impressionist art, or to the clashing colours of Post-Impressionism or Fauvism (this painting is contemporary with Derain's Collioure landscape: see p.20). Bold, unmodulated colour only became a feature of his art around 1910. Instead this kind of tonal painting and the rich, creamy brushwork have their origin in the work of Manet and John Singer Sargent; there is even a parallel with the eighteenth-century Scottish portraitist Raeburn, whose Edinburgh studio Peploe occupied from 1905.

John Duncan Fergusson 1874–1961 · Dieppe, 14 July 1905: Night 1905

Fergusson was born in Leith, near Edinburgh. He studied in Paris and made regular visits to France from the mid-1890s, eventually settling there from 1907 to 1914 and again in the 1930s. This painting of 1905, one of Fergusson's largest to date, is much indebted to Whistler's *Firework Nocturne* paintings, not only for its subject, but also in the reliance on tonal harmonies. A memorial exhibition of Whistler's work was held in Paris and London in 1905 and Fergusson may

well have seen this. The figure in grey with his back to us, left of centre, is the artist S.J. Peploe (see opposite): he and Fergusson met at the turn of the century and often went on painting trips together, particularly to France.

Oil on canvas, 76.8 × 76.8
Purchased 1978
GMA 1713

John Duncan Fergusson 1874–1961 · *Portrait of Anne Estelle Rice* 1908

Having spent several lengthy periods in France, Fergusson moved to Paris in 1907, teaching part-time at an independent art school, the Académie de la Palette. He got to know the Fauve artists, including Matisse, and adopted a similar style to theirs, using pure, bright colours and bold, rhythmic contours. The contrast between this painting and the Whistlerian tones of *Dieppe, 14 July 1905: Night* (see p.91) shows just how much Fergusson's work had developed in three years.

Anne Estelle Rice (1879–1959) was an American artist who was born near Philadelphia and moved to Paris in 1906. She worked as an illustrator for a Philadelphia magazine but was also a distinguished painter. Fergusson met her in the summer of 1906, before moving to Paris, and subsequently contributed illustrations to the same magazine. The two became close friends. Later, in 1911, Fergusson was appointed art editor of *Rhythm*, a new English language magazine devoted to contemporary literature and art; Rice also contributed drawings and articles.

Oil on board, 66.5 × 57.5
Purchased 1971
GMA 1247

Samuel John Peploe 1871–1935 · *Still Life* c.1913

Oil on canvas, 55 × 46
Presented by Mr A. J.
McNeill Reid 1946
GMA 32

Peploe made a number of portraits and figure paintings in his early years but after about 1910, the year he moved to Paris, he concentrated almost exclusively on still lifes and landscapes. In France his use of colour became much more daring, and he began to use more structured brushstrokes, in the manner of Van Gogh and Cézanne.

Peploe returned to live in Edinburgh in the summer of 1912. This painting was exhibited in Edinburgh the following year. Peploe was never as involved in avant-garde circles as was Fergusson, but this work shows his awareness of Cubist painting: a review of the 1913 exhibition mentions his 'daringly, vivid still life studies with a leaning to Cubism'. The angular contour lines, flattened perspective and suppressed shadows do hint at Cubism, but Peploe, like most Scottish artists of this period, was not tempted by abstraction.

John Quinton Pringle 1864–1925 · Poultry Yard, Gartcosh 1906

Born in Glasgow, Pringle was apprenticed to an optician and also took evening courses at Glasgow School of Art. He established his own optician and electrician's shop in Glasgow in 1896 and worked full-time there until his retirement in 1923. However, he continued to paint, mainly working early in the mornings and late at night. He seldom exhibited, painted comparatively few works (most of which are small in scale) and seems to have kept a deliberately low profile.

Pringle followed a manner employed by the Glasgow Boys (such as Guthrie, Lavery and Hornel), which in turn derived from French painting (especially Bastien-Lepage), of painting with small, square brushstrokes, rather than trying to make the strokes blend together. In the early 1900s he took this method a stage further, using tiny dabs of colour which seem to mix together optically when seen from a distance. This manner probably derived from the French Neo-Impressionists, though it is not clear where he might have seen their work. His training as an optician – and familiarity with very painstaking, detailed work – is also relevant. This painting, among Pringle's largest works, dates from the year he lived in Gartcosh, to the east of Glasgow.

Oil on canvas, 63.7 × 76.4
Presented by Mr James
Meldrum 1948
GMA 37

Francis Campbell Boileau Cadell 1883–1937 · *The Model* c.1912

Oil on canvas,
127.2 × 101.6
Purchased 1947
GMA 3

Born in Edinburgh, Cadell lived in Paris from 1899 to 1902, studying at the Académie Julian. Afterwards he remained based in Edinburgh, but went on regular summer trips to the Western Isles, often with Peploe, and also to France. Cadell's work owes much to the French Impressionists, though the influence was probably as much mediated through Peploe as it was experienced directly. His paintings of this period have a blond tonality, while the brushwork is lively and broad.

This is the largest of several paintings of the period (indeed it is one of Cadell's largest works) showing a nude model reflected in a mirror. The use of the mirror was a popular artistic conceit, enabling front and back views of the model to be represented in a single picture.

Until the creation of the Scottish National Gallery of Modern Art in 1959, the National Gallery of Scotland would not countenance the purchase of work by living artists or even those who had been dead less than ten years (exceptions were sometimes made with regard to gifts). This painting was bought immediately after Cadell's ten-year period in 'purgatory' had elapsed.

Oil on canvas, 76.3 × 63.5
Bequeathed by Mr and Mrs
G.D. Robinson through the
National Art Collections
Fund 1988
GMA 3350

After the war Cadell abandoned his feathery, Impressionistic manner (see p.95) for more geometric compositions and vivid, acidic colours. The brushwork is now scarcely visible and shadows have been suppressed to such an extent that the painting reads almost as a two-dimensional pattern.

The sitter in this painting is Berthia Hamilton Don-Wauchope (1864–1944), an Edinburgh model who posed regularly for Cadell (and is often pictured wearing a black hat) from about 1911 to 1926. Although she looks much younger, she would have been in her late fifties when the portrait was painted. The distinctive mauve-coloured walls indicate that the portrait was painted in Cadell's studio in Ainslie Place, Edinburgh, where the artist lived from 1920. Cadell often included the names of colours in the titles of his paintings: this practice, made popular by Whistler, became fashionable during the Edwardian period.

George Leslie Hunter 1877–1931 · *Reflections, Balloch c.1929–30*

Hunter was born on the Isle of Bute. His family emigrated to California in 1892 and by the turn of the century he was making a living there as an illustrator. Little is known of his early work since much of it was destroyed in the San Francisco earthquake of 1906. He moved to Glasgow soon afterwards.

During the 1920s Hunter emerged alongside Cadell, Fergusson and Peploe as one of a group of Scottish artists influenced by the pure, bright colour and loose brushwork of French Fauve painting (see p.20). While the other three 'Scottish Colourists' had spent extended periods in France, Hunter seems to have gone there only once or twice. However, in the 1920s he made several lengthy stays, living at St-Paul-de-Vence, near Nice, from 1927 to 1929. Impressed by the strong Mediterranean light, Hunter lightened his palette, and his handling of paint became bolder and more fluent.

In 1929 he fell ill and returned to Glasgow. Once recovered he embarked upon a series of paintings of Loch Lomond, north-west of Glasgow, and the village of Balloch which lies at its southern end. He had painted in the same area in 1924 but these new works reveal the lessons he had learned in the south of France and the influence in particular of Matisse.

Oil on canvas, 63.5 × 76.2
Presented by Mr William McInnes 1933
GMA 18

Duncan Grant 1885–1978 · Vanessa Bell Painting 1915

Oil on canvas, 76.2 × 55.9
Purchased 1965
GMA 900

Grant was born in Scotland but spent his childhood in Burma; he lived in England from 1895. He became one of the main figures of the Bloomsbury Group, a loosely-knit circle of mainly well-heeled artists, writers and intellectuals, resident in the Bloomsbury area of London in the years before the First World War. He was introduced to the group through his cousin, the writer Lytton Strachey, but had already met Vanessa Bell and her husband Clive, two pillars of the group, a few years earlier. Another Bloomsbury regular was the critic Roger Fry, whose espousal of French Post-Impressionism strongly influenced the others.

This work, which shows Vanessa Bell painting a still life of kitchen utensils, was executed in a boat-house at West Wittering on the Sussex coast in the early summer of 1915 (the date inscribed on the canvas, 1913, is incorrect). Friends had lent Bell and Grant a house in the village, and the artist Henry Tonks allowed them to use his nearby boat-house as a studio. By this date Vanessa had left both Clive Bell and Fry, with whom she had had a liaison.

A conscientious objector, Grant did agricultural work during the war and, with Bell and another friend, left London and moved into Charleston house, near Lewes in Sussex. Bell and Grant remained at Charleston until their deaths, transforming the house with their decorative wall-paintings and furniture.

Gwen John 1876–1939 · A Young Nun c.1915–20

Gwen John was the elder sister of the artist Augustus John (see p.101). For many years her brother's reputation overshadowed her own, though in recent years she has probably become the better known of the two.

She studied at the Slade School of Art in London and in 1904 settled in Paris. There she worked as a model, notably for the sculptor Auguste Rodin, with whom she had an affair. In 1913 she became a Catholic. About that time she received a commission from the convent of the Dominican Sisters of Charity at Meudon, near Paris, to paint the portrait of the nun who in 1696 had founded their order. The portrait took several years to complete, partly because a number of the nuns requested copies to hang in their own rooms. Concurrently, John worked for about twelve years on a series of uncommissioned portraits of the nuns. She painted the young nun in this picture (her name is not recorded) on at least one other occasion. The narrow tonal range, delicately textured surface and quiet sensitivity are typical of Gwen John's work.

Oil on canvas, 65.1 × 49
Purchased 1970
GMA 1116

Walter Richard Sickert 1860–1942 · High-Steppers c.1938

Oil on canvas, 132 × 122.5
Purchased 1979
GMA 2099

Sickert was born in Munich to parents of Danish origin but British national-ity. His work owes much to Degas, whom he met in Paris in 1881. Like Degas he sought apparently casual, accidental effects, and liked unusual lighting; he also employed a similar technique and chose similar subject matter, particularly theatre scenes.

In the late 1920s Sickert adopted the unorthodox practice of copying directly from photographs. He would select images from newspapers, square them up, and copy them onto a rough-textured canvas. He even had a photographer take shots of himself so that he could copy the photographs afterwards.

Sickert was interested in the stage from an early age and as a young man worked as an actor. *High-Steppers*, probably Sickert's last theatre painting, is his third of the Plaza Tiller Girls. All three versions were painted after a photograph which appeared in *The Evening News* in 1927. The first two versions were finished in 1928 and this third version followed some ten years later. Tiller Girls were the product of a dance school formed by John and Mary Tiller. Thirteen Tiller troupes operated in London, each performing at different theatres and cinemas: the Plaza Tiller girls danced at the Plaza cinema in Piccadilly, entertaining the audience before the start of the film. The photograph showed the troupe performing their routine at Elstree studios in 1927, probably for a film called *A Little Bit of Fluff*.

Matthew Smith 1879–1959 · *Portrait of Augustus John* 1944

Smith was born in Halifax and studied at the Slade School of Art in London from 1905 to 1908. He then lived in France for six years, briefly attending Matisse's art school in Paris. In the 1920s and 1930s he spent part of each year in France.

Smith is chiefly known for his richly coloured, sensuous nudes and still lifes, but he also painted a number of portraits, most of which date from his later years. When the Second World War broke out Smith was forced to abandon his studio in the south of France, and early in the war his two sons were killed in action. Deeply depressed, he virtually stopped painting. In 1944 he spent several months with his great friend Augustus John at Freyern Court, on the edge of the New Forest, and prompted by John and his wife Dorelia he began to paint again.

This is one of four portraits Smith made of John in October 1944: it was allegedly painted in under an hour. Alluding to Smith's penchant for painting flesh as if it had been flayed and soaked in blood, John jokingly referred to the painting as 'Another haemorrhage for Matthew; all the same he will be a portrait painter yet.' John also painted Smith, and when Smith was told that his painting was better, he remarked, 'Ah, but I had by far the more interesting subject!'

Oil on canvas, 102.3 × 77
Purchased 1981
GMA 2324

Gill was born in Brighton where his father was a clergyman in a small Calvinist sect. Later his father joined the Church of England, becoming a curate at Chichester, further west along the Sussex coast. Gill enrolled at a local art school at the age of fifteen, and being the son of a clergyman had free access to Chichester's great medieval cathedral, where his passion for calligraphy and masonry was nurtured.

He moved to London in 1900 to join an architectural practice and soon afterwards enrolled in evening classes, where he learned masonry, calligraphy and letter-carving. In 1903 he abandoned his architectural studies and set up as a letter-cutter. Until the end of 1909 all Gill's carved work was in the form of lettering, or occasionally decorative mouldings, but he then began to make three-dimensional, figurative sculptures. Contrary to the conventional practice of modelling sculptures in clay and having specialists carve them in stone, Gill did all his own carving.

His first crucifix (now in the Tate Gallery, London) dates from 1909–10. In the next couple of years he moved close to Catholicism, converting in 1913. *Christ on the Cross* dates from that year. In August 1913 Gill was invited to carve a series of Stations of the Cross for Westminster Cathedral in London, a commission which took several years to complete.

Hoptonwood stone, partly painted,
31.2 × 14 × 3.5
Bequeathed by Sir David Young Cameron 1945
GMA 14

Henri Gaudier-Brzeska 1891–1915 · *Bird Swallowing a Fish* 1914

Henri Gaudier was born near Orléans in France. In 1910 he met a Polish woman, Sophie Brzeska, and though they did not marry they joined their names together. They moved to London in 1911.

During 1913 and 1914 Gaudier-Brzeska established close links with the leading figures in London's literary and artistic avant-garde, including Wyndham Lewis and Epstein. He was an original member of Lewis's Vorticist group (see p.104), which was launched in the summer of 1914 in the form of a stirring publication called *Blast*. By the age of twenty-three, Gaudier-Brzeska had become one of the most radical sculptors working in Britain. *Bird Swallowing a Fish* exemplifies his search for an art fusing mechanical and organic forms. Modelled and carved in plaster, it is one of his last sculptures and probably dates from late spring 1914. It was exhibited in London in June of that year, cast in gun-metal; our version is a posthumous bronze cast. The aggressive subject and form and the torpedo-like shape of the fish, seem like portents of war, which already looked inevitable by spring 1914 and was declared in July. Shortly afterwards Gaudier-Brzeska left Britain to join the French army. He was killed in action in June 1915.

Bronze, 32 × 60.5 × 29.5
Purchased 1980
GMA 2150

Oil on canvas, 165.2 × 90.2
Purchased 1977
GMA 1685

Lewis was born on his father's yacht off the Canadian coast. His father was American, his mother British; the family moved to England in 1888. Painter, poet and polemicist, in 1914 Lewis founded the Vorticist movement, a British hybrid of Cubism and Futurism. His work of this date verged on abstraction. The Vorticist movement petered out during the war but Lewis continued to produce provocative images throughout the 1920s. From 1920 to 1921 he embarked upon a series of portraits of 'Tyros', which he exhibited in London in April 1921; he also published two issues of a magazine called *The Tyro*. Tyro means a 'novice' or 'beginner', but Lewis expanded upon this definition, calling him 'a new type of human animal like Harlequin or Punchinello ... The Tyro is raw and underdeveloped; his vitality is immense, but purposeless, and hence sometimes malignant. His keynote, however, is vacuity, he is an animated but artificial puppet, a "novice" to real life ... '

Lewis made a series of these satirical tyro paintings: *A Reading of Ovid* is one of the largest and most important. He wrote: 'The "Tyros Reading Ovid" ... is one of the paintings I took longest over, is very carefully painted ... it would make a good altarpiece.' Lewis had a strong personality and was often critical of his contemporaries. He described the *Tyros* series as a satire, 'a challenge to the Arts-for-Arts-sake dilettantism of a great deal of French work of to-day (and the Bloomsbury Bell-Grant-Fry section of English).'

William Roberts 1895–1980 · *The Rhine Boat c.1928*

Born in London, Roberts joined the Vorticist group (see opposite) in 1914, and like Wyndham Lewis painted in a machine-orientated style, verging on abstraction. During the First World War he served as an official War Artist for the Canadian War Records Office (as did Lewis and Bomberg) and at that time he began to adopt a more naturalistic approach.

In the 1920s Roberts abandoned the hard, machine-like angularity associated with Vorticism for an equally stylized but more legible form of narrative painting. The style owes much to the highly formalised manner adopted by Fernand Léger (see p.33) and his circle, sometimes referred to – for obvious reasons – as 'Tubism'. Many of Roberts's paintings from this date feature people engaged in ordinary social activities such as playing, relaxing and working. He would establish the composition in drawings, creating strong formal rhythms and rhymes, and would then square these up and methodically transfer the design on to canvas.

Roberts went on a boat trip down the river Rhine in the summer of 1928 and this painting was probably made soon after his return.

Oil on canvas, 50.8 × 40.6
Presented by Miss Elizabeth Watt 1961
GMA 783

Epstein was born in New York. He studied art in Paris and then settled in England in 1905. By 1920 he had become probably the most notorious modern artist working in Britain, vilified for the stylised treatment of form in some works and for the brazen nudity in others.

The Risen Christ was begun as a portrait of Epstein's friend, the composer Bernard van Dieren. Epstein started it in 1917 when van Dieren was ill and later recalled: 'Watching his head, so spiritual and worn with suffering, I thought I would like to make a mask of him. I hurried home and returned with clay and made a mask which I immediately recognised as the Christ head, with its short beard, its pitying accusing eyes, and the lofty and broad brow ... I saw the whole figure of my "Christ" in the mask. With haste I began to add the torso and the arms and hand with the accusing finger ... So far the work was a bust. I then set up this bust with an armature for the body. I established the length of the whole figure down to the feet. The statue rose swathed in clothes.' He had to call a halt to work late in 1917 when he was enlisted, but continued on it a year later. Other friends posed for the unfinished parts. Epstein considered the figure an anti-war statement and declared that 'I should like to re-model this "Christ". I should like to make it hundreds of feet high, and set it up on some high place where all could see it, and where it would give out its warning, its mighty symbolic warning to all lands.' *The Risen Christ* is a unique bronze cast.

Bronze, 218.5 × 54.5 × 56
Purchased 1969
GMA 1092

Epstein was one of the first sculptors to take an interest in African and Oceanic art, and he had an outstanding collection of his own. The strong, direct character of such works had a major influence on his style of carving. Like Brancusi, Moore, Hepworth and many other early twentieth-century sculptors, Epstein wanted his carvings to reflect the individual qualities and form of the original block of stone. This tendency is often referred to as being 'true to the materials'.

In his autobiography, Epstein recalled that the idea for *Consummatum Est* came when he was looking at a huge slab of alabaster in his studio, and listening to Bach's B minor Mass:

'In the section "Crucifixus" I have a feeling of tremendous quiet, of awe. The music comes from a great distance and in this mood I conceive my *Consummatum Est*. I see the figure complete as a whole. I see immediately the upturned hands, with the wounds in the feet, stark, crude, with the stigmata.'

According to St John's Gospel, Consummatum Est – 'It is finished' – were the words Christ uttered from the cross. As was the case with *The Risen Christ*, the sculpture provoked a storm of protest when it was first exhibited in 1937. For years it belonged to Tussaud's fairground in Blackpool, where it was exhibited as a curiosity, alongside other Epstein carvings.

Alabaster, 61 × 223.5 × 81
Purchased 1981
GMA 2304

William McCance 1894–1970 · Portrait of Joseph Brewer 1925

McCance was born in the south of Glasgow and studied at Glasgow School of Art from 1911 to 1915. In 1918 he married a fellow student, Agnes Miller Parker (one of Britain's leading wood-engravers), and they moved to London two years later. In the early 1920s McCance developed a machine-like, near abstract style, much indebted to the work of Wyndham Lewis and the Vorticists (see p.104). He was one of very few Scottish artists to follow such a path. From 1923 to 1926 he worked as art critic for *The Spectator* magazine, for which the American Joseph Brewer, portrayed in this painting, acted as secretary to the editor. The vivid colours, metallic sheen and sculptural, robotic forms, are typical of McCance's work of this period.

Many of McCance's paintings and drawings show figures reading, which may reflect his own work as a writer, his keen intellectual spirit, and his interest in book design. From 1930 to 1933 he worked as controller of the celebrated Gregynog Press in Wales, where leading British printmakers and typographers produced highly prized, limited edition books. He later taught typography and book design at Reading University before retiring to Scotland in 1963.

Oil on canvas, 76.3 × 61.3
Purchased 1989
GMA 3446

David Bomberg 1890–1957 · *Self-Portrait* 1937

Born in Birmingham, Bomberg grew up in London's East End. He studied at the Slade School of Art. Having seen Roger Fry's celebrated exhibition of Post-Impressionist art in London in 1910, Bomberg was soon painting large, near-abstract paintings, based on Cubist grid patterns. Fiercely independent, he rebuffed Lewis's invitation to join the Vorticist group, though he did once exhibit with them.

After the war (indeed, partly because of it) his work underwent a volte-face and he began to make detailed landscape paintings. He visited Spain in 1929 and lived there from 1934 to 1935, only returning to London when civil war seemed imminent. This dark, brooding self-portrait was painted in Hampstead in 1937. That year Bomberg suffered a series of setbacks leading to deep depression. The Tate Gallery declined to acquire any of his works for their collection; his financial worries mounted; the situation in Nazi Germany became increasingly black, with Jewish artists forbidden to exhibit; and the Civil War in his beloved Spain was raging. Bomberg, who was Jewish, became actively involved in anti-fascist activities. His wife recalled: 'David was depressed day after day reading *The Times*, so I suggested that he paint himself in the back room which had a skylight.' The series of introspective self-portraits of 1937 are direct reflections of his anxiety.

Oil on canvas, 77.2 × 56.5
Purchased (Knapping Fund)
1967
GMA 994

Ben Nicholson 1894–1982 · *Walton Wood Cottage, No.I* 1928

Oil on canvas, 56 × 61
Presented by Miss Helen
Sutherland 1965
GMA 930

Ben Nicholson was the eldest son of the painters William Nicholson and Mabel Pryde (see p.88). He married Winifred Roberts (see opposite) in 1920 and in the next ten years they divided their time between London, Switzerland and Cumberland, and also made occasional visits to Paris.

Winifred's family had lived in Cumberland for generations and in 1924 the couple bought a house at Bankshead, on the Roman wall. Friends such as Paul Nash, Ivon Hitchens and Christopher Wood stayed there. Ben Nicholson rejected the dark tones favoured by the Edwardians for light, fresh colours and a deliberately naïve approach. His work verged on abstraction during 1924, but for the rest of the decade he reaffirmed his subject matter – almost exclusively landscape and still-life motifs. This painting is the first of two showing a cottage at Walton Wood near Bankshead. The cottage (which no longer exists) was one of several belonging to Winifred Roberts's grandfather, the Earl of Carlisle. It was rented at the time by Robert Graves, who was married to Ben Nicholson's sister, Nancy.

Even in this, an early work, Nicholson's interest in space, clarity and natural materials is evident. The underlying green colour seems to have been wiped on with a sponge or rag rather than applied with a brush, and suggests the circulation of cool air. A debt to Cubism is apparent in the way flat blocks of colour structure the surface of the picture, but there are also parallels with the simple compositions favoured by Ben's father, William.

Winifred Nicholson 1893–1981 · *Jake and Kate on the Isle of Wight* 1931–32

Winifred Roberts and Ben Nicholson were married in 1920 but separated in 1931, when Ben went to live with the sculptor Barbara Hepworth. Winifred took charge of their three young children, Jake, Kate and Andrew. Feeling the need for new surroundings, she rented a house at Fishbourne on the Isle of Wight in the winter of 1931/32. This picture was painted there and shows Jake and Kate (Andrew was only a few months old) in the conservatory, which looks out on to the Solent; their party hats indicate that it may be Christmas-time. The ship seen in the distance was once thought to be the luxury French liner the *Normandie*, and until recently the painting was always titled *Jake, Kate and the Normandie*. However, that vessel was only launched in 1935 and it may instead be a German ship such as the *Bremen* or *Europa*, or it may equally be

an invented element. Another version of the painting, without the ship, is in Bristol Museum and Art Gallery.

The delicate, fresh colours and appealing naïvety are typical of Winifred Nicholson's work. The painting offers an interesting contrast to Orpen's *A Bloomsbury Family*, which shows the previous generation of Nicholson children (see p.88).

Oil on canvas, 68.5 × 89
Presented by the Trustees of
Winifred Nicholson's estate
in accordance with her
wishes 1985
GMA 2964

Christopher Wood 1901–30 · Nude Boy in a Bedroom 1930

Wood was born near Liverpool and studied architecture before turning to painting. Following a spell in London he moved to Paris in 1921. He met Picasso, developed friendships with the poets Jean Cocteau and Max Jacob, and was extremely productive, painting some 500 oils in his short career.

In 1926 he met Ben and Winifred Nicholson (see pp.110–111) who became close friends and whose fresh, *faux-naïf* style of painting influenced his own. He stayed in Brittany in the summers of 1929 and 1930. This painting was executed in June or July 1930 when he lodged at the hotel Ty-Mad in Tréboul, near the tip of Brittany, with Jacob and the designer Christian Bérard. The 'boy' is one of Wood's many lovers, the artist Francis Rose. Through Cocteau's circle Wood had been introduced to opium smoking – and later opium eating – which affected his mental stability: this problematic side to Wood's character sometimes surfaces in his art. The tarot cards lying on the bed are the Pentacles, the Nave of Ones and the Swords (or Threes). They appear in the same formation in another painting and can be interpreted in a number of ways. They may allude to worries about money and love and also to danger; in any event, they seem to tell of his troubled state of mind. A few months later Wood was killed by a train. Whether it was suicide, an accident, drug related or the result of mental instability, remains unclear.

The painting formerly belonged to the actor John Gielgud.

Oil on hardboard laid on plywood, 53.8 × 65. Purchased 1978
GMA 1712

Anne Redpath 1895–1965 · *The Indian Rug c.1942*

Having studied at Edinburgh College of Art, Redpath married and in 1920 went to live in France, where her husband worked as an architect with the War Graves Commission. She brought up a family and painted comparatively little until the mid-1930s when she returned to Scotland, settling in Hawick in the Borders. *The Indian Rug* is a fairly early work from this second phase in her career. The vivid colours and decorative sense of form owe much to Matisse, whose work Redpath no doubt encountered in France, but the 'tipped-up' perspective also reflects her great admiration for early Italian painting. The pattern of the rug mixes with the 'real' slippers and chair to such a degree that it is difficult to disengage flat from three-dimensional form. Redpath's father designed tweed fabrics and her work

does also have the sense of patterning sometimes found in textiles. She herself remarked: 'I do with a spot of red or yellow in a harmony of grey what my father did with his tweed.' Exhibited with the title *The Indian Rug* at Redpath's retrospective exhibition of 1965, this painting is probably identical with a work entitled *Red Slippers* which was shown at the Royal Scottish Academy in Edinburgh in 1942.

*Oil on plywood, 73.9 × 96.1
Purchased 1965
GMA 932*

113

James Cowie 1886–1956 · A Portrait Group 1933 / c.1940

Oil on canvas,
101.6 × 127.3
Purchased 1975
GMA 1325

It is often said that Glasgow students painted in a precise, linear manner, while Edinburgh students adopted a freer, more painterly style. Cowie, who was born in Aberdeenshire and studied at Glasgow School of Art from 1912 to 1914, was one of the leading Scottish artists of this hard, linear style. He taught at Bellshill Academy, near Glasgow, until 1935. A Portrait Group was originally painted in 1933 and featured four of the Bellshill pupils. A photograph records its appearance at that date.

In 1937 Cowie became Warden at Hospitalfield House, an art school near Arbroath, and in about 1940 he reworked the painting. The alterations he made are intriguing and difficult to account for. The most dramatic

change is to the female figure in the foreground who has been transformed from a schoolgirl into a mature woman. The reworked head is based on a friend whose portrait Cowie had painted in 1935. Strategically placed on the table next to her are two ripe fruit. The table cloth has changed from one with a striped design to a squared pattern, while the stripes on the right have been repainted in a slightly different way. Other new details include the hanging drapery and a building based upon his uncle's farm. Close comparison between the old photograph and the picture as it now stands shows that Cowie repainted almost every detail.

James McIntosh Patrick 1907–98 · *Traquair House* 1938

James McIntosh Patrick was born in Dundee and studied at Glasgow School of Art from 1924 to 1928. By his mid-twenties he had won national recognition as a printmaker of highly detailed landscape panoramas and townscapes. When the print market slumped in the early 1930s he resumed oil painting, mainly choosing landscapes in and around the Dundee area. These paintings are executed with a fastidious attention to detail, but McIntosh Patrick would often rearrange the topography, shifting mountains, changing scale, and altering perspective for pictorial ends.

This painting is one of several executed in the late 1930s which show large Scottish houses or castles. It depicts Traquair House, near Peebles, south of Edinburgh (the house is substantially seventeenth-century though it has much earlier parts). The artist and his family regularly spent their holidays in the Peebles area in the 1930s. According to his usual practice, McIntosh Patrick made sketches and watercolours at Traquair House and used these as the basis for the oil painting, which was executed in his Dundee studio.

Oil on canvas, 35.5 × 45.5
Purchased 1990
GMA 3534

Oil on canvas, 76.5 × 91.5
Bequeathed by Dr R.A. Lillie
1977
GMA 1766

Born in Haddington, Gillies studied at Edinburgh College of Art. He is the exemplar of the painterly approach associated with the College. As a teacher there for more than forty years until his retirement as Principal in 1966, he influenced several generations of artists.

A College grant enabled Gillies to go to Paris in 1923 and study under the Cubist painter André Lhote, and for a brief period he worked in a Cubist style. But by nature he was more inclined to the *belle peinture* tradition, and he quickly shrugged off the Cubist influence. His oeuvre is equally split between landscapes and still lifes and between oil paintings and watercolours. This work depicts the harbour at Anstruther, on the Fife coast. An exhibition of Paul Klee's work (see p.55) took place in Edinburgh in 1934 and this work seems to reflect the childlike characteristics of Klee's art, as well as Klee's practice of dividing the space into a flat, grid-like composition.

The Gallery owns more than 170 paintings and watercolours by Gillies, most of them bequeathed by the collector Dr Robert Lillie.

John Maxwell 1905–62 · *View from a Tent* 1933

Maxwell was born in Dalbeattie, Kirkcudbrightshire. He attended Edinburgh College of Art from 1921 to 1926 and then travelled in Europe for a year. For a short period he, like several other Scottish artists of his generation, studied in Paris under Léger and another artist of the Cubist school, Amedée Ozenfant.

In 1929 Maxwell was given a part-time teaching post at Edinburgh College of Art and in 1933 was awarded a two-year Fellowship at the College. *View from a Tent* dates from that year and was painted during a trip he and William Gillies (see opposite), also a teacher at the College of Art, made to the Highlands. It depicts the sands of Morar, on the west coast of Scotland, glimpsed from the inside of

the tent they shared. Gillies had painted in the area in previous years but this was the first time they had painted there together. Gillies later recalled: 'Whenever I see a photo or picture of Morar, it conjures up our first trip together to the West and I see again that lovely painting of Morar sands enclosed in the flaps of our tent.'

Maxwell later said that the trips with Gillies were a mixed blessing, for although he enjoyed the latter's company, he was intimidated by the speed at which Gillies worked: Gillies could finish half a dozen watercolours before he had even selected a motif.

Oil on plywood,
76.2 × 91.5
Purchased 1966
GMA 977

Edward Wadsworth 1889–1949 · *Composition, Crank and Chain* 1932

Wadsworth was born in Yorkshire. He was one of the original members of Wyndham Lewis's Vorticist movement (see p.104), and was among the first British artists to adopt a machine-orientated type of abstraction. He visited France regularly in the 1920s, and was influenced by artists such as Léger and also by the Surrealists. Like Tristram Hillier (see opposite) he was particularly drawn to nautical themes, composing bizarre still lifes in beach settings. A devotee of early Italian painting, he preferred tempera to conventional oil paint.

In the early 1930s Wadsworth returned to abstraction, but moved away from the hard, aggressive style of his Vorticist period to forms which seem almost biological in inspiration. This type of work owed much to Léger and his followers. For many modern artists, scientific discoveries of a microscopic, biological nature, were as stimulating, and as indicative of the modern spirit as new developments in machinery or industry. Wadsworth was in close contact with developments in the French avant-garde, travelling to France regularly and exhibiting there. On the Continent he was recognised, in the early 1930s, as probably Britain's leading abstract artist.

Tempera on board, 35 × 40
Presented by Mr and Mrs J.
H. Macdonell 1960
GMA 768

Tristram Hillier 1905–83 · *Pylons* 1933

Hillier was born in China but his family moved to England soon after his birth. He was a member of the Unit One group, which was launched in 1933 by Paul Nash and included Ben Nicholson, Moore and Hepworth among its members. Inspired by European abstraction and Surrealism, the group was the most radical British art movement of the period, though it folded in 1935. *Pylons* was exhibited at the first and only Unit One exhibition in London in 1934, where it aroused much interest. It was purchased from the exhibition by Elizabeth Watt, who bequeathed it to the Gallery more than fifty years later.

Hillier was strongly influenced by Cubism and Surrealism but stated in 1934: 'Generally my aim is to build up a composition in a representative manner, assembling objects which have a mutual plastic complement and a similar evocative nature irrespective of their individual functions. Unlike Monsieur Dali I have no wish to shock people's sensibilities by juxtaposing the most unlikely objects in an improbable landscape setting.'

Pylons had both positive and negative connotations: they seemed menacing and ugly, yet could improve the lives of millions. The Central Electricity Board's national grid was completed in 1933, by which date nearly 4,000 pylons had been erected in Britain. In this painting the three tall vertical pylons carry no wires and their location on the beach is deliberately enigmatic.

Oil on canvas, 92 × 60.3
Bequeathed by Miss Elizabeth Watt 1989
GMA 3488

Oil on canvas,
137.2 × 243.8
Presented by Mrs Hope
Montagu Douglas Scott
1971
GMA 1254

The son of a farmer, Johnstone was born in Roxburghshire. Having attended Edinburgh College of Art, in 1925 he went to Paris where he studied under the Cubist painter André Lhote. His work of the late 1920s combines influences from Cubism, Surrealism and abstraction and is unique in Scottish art; indeed, it has few parallels with the work of any of his contemporaries. Johnstone recalled that he began A Point in Time in 1929 when he was living in Selkirk. It is his largest painting of this period and the artist emphasised its importance by taking its title for his autobiography. He said that A Point in Time and two other large paintings of the period 'grew out of my horror of the disease of war, of the anticipation of future tragedy – they were never intended for drawing rooms.' Johnstone reworked many of his paintings of the 1920s and A Point in Time was probably altered prior to its first exhibition in 1938. A small oil study for the painting is also in the Gallery's collection.

In 1931 Johnstone settled in London where he pursued a successful teaching career, becoming Principal of Camberwell School of Arts and Crafts and latterly Principal of the Central School. He was responsible for giving a number of young artists their first official teaching posts – for example Davie, Paolozzi and Turnbull (see pp.154–157 and 166). He retired in 1960 and returned to the Scottish Borders to farm.

John Piper 1903–92 · Black Ground (or Screen for the Sea) 1938

Piper was born in Surrey and studied at the Royal College of Art in London. He is best known for his picturesque, architectural and landscape paintings, which are in the Romantic tradition of Blake, Palmer and Turner, but for a brief period in the 1930s his paintings were abstract. *Black Ground*, one of Piper's last abstract works (and one of his largest ever works), was exhibited in 1938 with the title *Screen for the Sea*, though he changed the title some years later. It clearly refers to the Cubist compositions of Braque and Picasso, and is closely related to a mural Piper did for a friend's flat in Highgate, London, in 1938.

Just as Paul Nash experimented briefly with abstraction, then returned to landscape painting, so too did Piper. In 1937 he wrote a veiled attack on the vogue for abstraction in an essay titled 'Lost, a Valuable Object', and in 1938 he again defended subject matter, in an article called 'Abstraction on the Beach'. He wrote that: 'Pure abstraction is undernourished. It should at least be allowed to feed on a bare beach with tins and broken bottles'. The abstracted motifs represented in this picture are a bottle and a stringed instrument, and the reference in the painting's title to the sea suggests that it may have originated in a seascape.

Oil on canvas, 121.6 × 182.8
Purchased 1978
GMA 1998

Ben Nicholson 1894–1982 · *White Relief* 1935

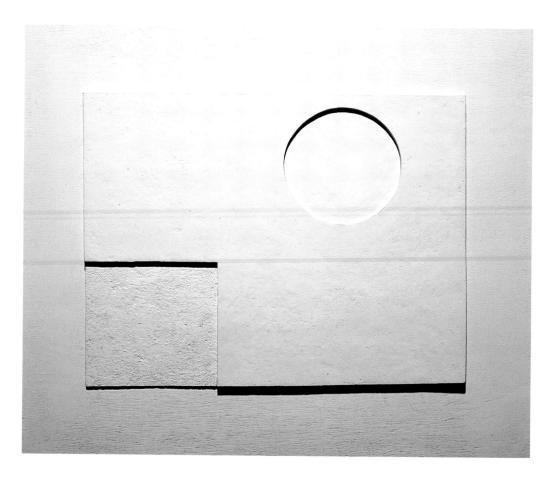

Oil on carved board,
54 × 64.3
Purchased 1980
GMA 2149

Nicholson's first relief painting was made on a trip to Paris in 1933. While working on a painting, part of the thick white ground chipped off, leaving two distinct layers. He exploited this accident in a series of white reliefs made in the mid- to late 1930s, and he continued to produce such reliefs throughout his career. They were made by sticking layers of board onto one another and also by carving into the surface. From the late 1930s he added colour and graphic marks. These works relate to the purity of Mondrian's works (Nicholson visited Mondrian's studio in 1934), and also to contemporary 'International Style' buildings by architects such as Le Corbusier. Nicholson was closely associated with leading British modernist architects of the period, indeed his brother Kit was a noted architect. His friendships with Barbara Hepworth (they were married in 1934) and Henry Moore may also have prompted this move into three-dimensional art.

Naum Gabo 1890–1977 · *Spiral Theme* 1941

Gabo was born in Russia and trained in Munich as a scientist and engineer. Of an intellectual disposition, he was influenced in a general way by scientists such as Einstein who were developing new ways of understanding space, time and matter. In order to give form to these ideas, Gabo rejected traditional, solid materials such as bronze and stone, and in the early 1920s began using transparent plastics. These enabled him to open up the form, unite solid and void and make space an active ingredient in his sculpture.

Gabo lived in England from 1936 to 1946, forming close friendships with Moore, Nicholson and Hepworth, and influencing the work of all three: incorporating string into sculpture, which Hepworth and Moore did, was

his idea. *Spiral Theme* is one of four small models which precede two much larger versions. They were all made when Gabo was living near St Ives in Cornwall. The plastic materials were provided by a friend who worked for Imperial Chemical Industries (ICI).

The *Spiral Theme* works proved to be among Gabo's most successful. In 1942 the critic Herbert Read referred to one of the large versions as 'the highest point ever reached by the aesthetic intuition of man'. Gabo was delighted by the reception it received: 'To my complete surprise this object has produced, what I would describe as, a tremendous effect on the mass of visitors ... Why is it precisely this spiral construction that has hit a nail on the head ... ? Probably I'll never be able to explain this.'

Celluloid on perspex base,
7 × 15.9 × 15.9
Purchased 1986
GMA 2978

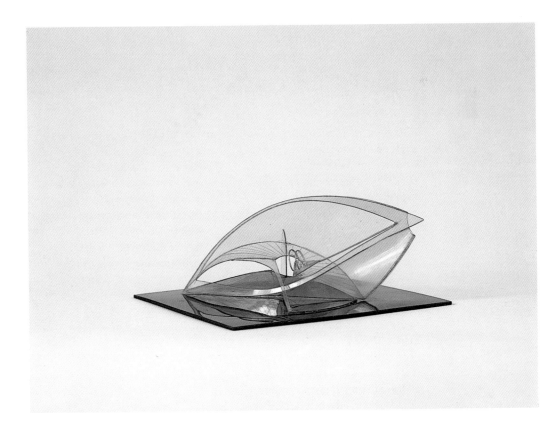

Roland Penrose 1900–84 · Untitled 1937

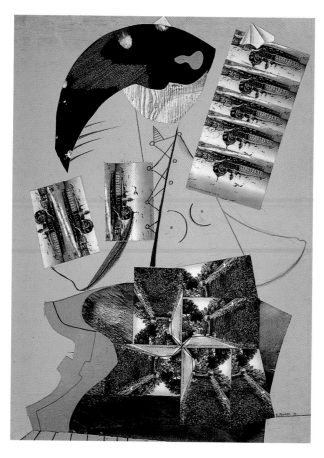

Collage, gouache and pencil on card, 80.5 × 54.5
Bequeathed by Gabrielle Keiller 1995
GMA 4070

Born in London into a well-to-do artistic family (his father was a painter), Penrose studied at Cambridge University. He moved to Paris in 1922, studying under André Lhote. Through Max Ernst, whom he met in 1925, Penrose was introduced to members of the Surrealist group, and also to Picasso, who became a good friend. Penrose was one of the principal organisers of the International Surrealist Exhibition, held in London in 1936, and after the war he organised numerous exhibitions for the Tate Gallery and the Institute of Contemporary Arts, which he co-founded. During the 1930s Penrose formed the finest private collection of Cubist and Surrealist art ever to be assembled in Britain. More than thirty items from his collection now belong to the Gallery (see for example pp.29–30, 54, 65 (both), 69 (bottom), 70–71, 72 (left), 73–74, 76, 78, 79 (top), 81 (bottom), 84, 128, 133 and 135), including a group of Surrealist works bought in 1995 with help from the Heritage Lottery Fund and National Art Collections Fund. His library and archive also belong to the Gallery.

Penrose was also a prolific artist. This is one of his earliest collages in which the image is constructed from postcards. He later wrote: 'Attracted by the vivid colour of the picture postcards on sale everywhere, I began to experiment with them in collages. Sometimes I found that repetitive clusters could take the effect of a spread of feathers or a single image cut out and set at a peculiar angle could transform completely its original meaning.'

Eileen Agar 1899–1991 · *Fish Circus* 1939

Agar was born in Buenos Aires into a wealthy family; her father was Scottish and her mother American. She went to school in England and studied at the Slade School of Art. Rebelling against her cloistered upbringing, she left her husband and in 1929 moved to Paris with her lover, the writer Joseph Bard. In Paris she continued painting and developed a particular interest in fossils. In 1935 she stayed near Swanage, on the Dorset coast, and there met Paul Nash (see p.127). Like him she began to compose works from found objects (*objets trouvés*) using the flotsam and jetsam washed up on the shore. Assemblages and collages of this kind became popular among the Surrealist group in the 1930s (see

p.84). Through Nash, Agar met Roland Penrose (see opposite), who included her work in the celebrated International Surrealist Exhibition held in London in 1936. Agar preferred, however, to remain distant from the theoretical and dogmatic aspects of Surrealism.

Agar and Bard usually spent their holidays by the sea, often in Dorset, Cornwall, the Channel Islands or on the French Riviera (in 1937 they holidayed with Picasso, Man Ray, Penrose and others at Mougins). This work, which is dated 1939, may have been made in the spring of that year, when they stayed near Toulon on the Mediterranean coast. It features a real starfish, pinned on with a thumbtack, together with collaged and drawn elements.

Collage, pen and ink and watercolour on paper, 21 × 26 (laid on paper, 25.5 × 30.5)
Bequeathed by Gabrielle Keiller 1995
GMA 3938

Graham Sutherland 1903–80 · *Western Hills* 1938/41

Oil on canvas, 55.5 × 90.5
Purchased 1967
GMA 1072

Sutherland studied at Goldsmiths' College, London, where he specialised in etching; he only began painting when he was in his late twenties. In 1934 he made the first of what would become regular visits to Pembrokeshire in Wales. The landscape there provided inspiration for many paintings and drawings, some of which reveal an interest in Surrealism. He made several paintings and studies of hills at Clegyr-Boia, on the western-most tip of Wales. Commenting on this landscape Sutherland wrote that: 'One approaches across a wide plain from the north ... One soon notices ... what appear to be two mountains. As one approaches closer one sees that these masses of rock scarcely attain a height of more than seven hundred feet. But so classically perfect is their form ... and so majestic is their command of the smoothly-rising ground below, that the mind ... holds their essential

mountainous significance.'

Western Hills was originally painted in 1938, sold, then returned to the artist in exchange for another painting. Sutherland reworked it in 1941 and remarked: 'It came back to me and caused me to feel that, though I still liked the composition, it lacked "body" in certain places. These I attempted to repaint, and, becoming very interested and absorbed, I completely repainted the whole picture, producing something absolutely different and bearing, I think, the fruits of thinking and feeling which has strongly attracted me during intervals during my war pictures.'

Paul Nash 1889–1946 · *Landscape of the Vernal Equinox (III)* 1944

From 1909 onwards the Nash family spent regular holidays with relatives living near Wallingford in Berkshire. Hills known as Wittenham Clumps were nearby. Nash described the Clumps as 'a landmark for miles around. An ancient British Camp, it stood up with extraordinary prominence ... There were two hills, both dome-like and each planted with a thick clump of trees whose mass had a curiously symmetrical sculptured form ... Ever since I remember them the Clumps had meant something to me. I felt their importance long before I knew their history. '

He first drew the Clumps in 1912. Towards the end of his life, when he was suffering from crippling asthma, he often stayed with friends at Sandlands, near Oxford, and from the garden he could see the Clumps in the far distance. He painted them in a series of dream-like works, three of which present the vernal equinox, with the sun and moon depicted simultaneously in the sky. These paintings were intended as poetic metaphors, referring to the mystery and magic of the perpetual cycles of nature. They were also symbolic in view of Nash's terminal illness, with the rising moon, casting a grey-violet light, replacing the falling sun. This, the last of the three versions, was painted for Margaret Nash, the artist's wife.

Oil on canvas, 63.5 × 76.2
Purchased 1961
GMA 774

Made during the early months of the Second World War, *The Helmet* is an important work in Moore's oeuvre since it is the first in a long series of sculptures to feature a form enclosed within another. A strange figure stands inside the helmet which is half-protective and half-menacing. Moore described the helmet motif as 'one form inside another, so you get the mystery of not entirely knowing the form inside … it's rather like armour which protects – the outer shell protecting the softer shell inside.'

The sculpture grew out of a number of themes. It relates to Moore's mother-and-child drawings in which the child is protected by the mother's arms; and to his drawings of shells, in which a complex internal structure is contained within a simpler outer form. Moore was also involved with Surrealism at this period, and the idea of the mind being an independent 'being' contained within a head finds expression here. However, the specific imagery in *The Helmet* derives from two sources. In 1939 Moore made a print of a Spanish Republican prisoner, his head rendered as a cage-like form behind a barbed-wire fence; and earlier, in 1937, he had made studies of an ancient Greek helmet with eye-like holes pierced in the top. These various ideas meet together in *The Helmet*, one of Moore's most complex and richly metaphorical works.

Lead, 29.1 × 18 × 16.5
Purchased with assistance
from the National Heritage
Memorial Fund, the
National Art Collections
Fund (Scottish Fund) and
the Henry Moore
Foundation 1992
GMA 3602

Watercolour, ink, wax crayon and chalk on paper, 52.3 × 44.9
Purchased 1978
GMA 2065

Two subjects dominate Moore's work: the reclining figure and mother-and-child groups. He began representing mothers holding their infants in the early 1920s, both in drawings and in sculptures. The theme assumed a new prominence in his work in the 1940s, following the commission in 1942 to carve a *Madonna and Child* for St Matthew's church in Northampton.

In 1944 Moore made a series of drawings and maquettes of family groups. These were preliminary ideas for a sculpture to be sited outside a school at Impington near Cambridge (the architect of the school was Walter Gropius). In several of the studies, two children are shown handling a book, a detail inspired by the scholastic nature of the project. The commission for the Impington sculpture had to be abandoned for financial reasons, but the project was revived a few years later when Moore was asked to make a sculpture for a secondary school at Stevenage, Hertfordshire. Inaugurated in 1949, that sculpture (his first large bronze) features the mother, father and a single child.

Barbara Hepworth 1903–75 · Dyad 1949

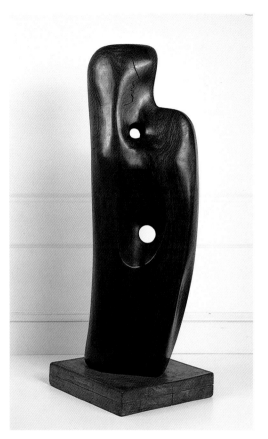 

Himalayan rosewood,
118 × 40.5 × 22
Purchased 1963
GMA 854

Hepworth was born in Wakefield, Yorkshire, and entered the Royal College of Art in London in 1921, as did Yorkshireman Henry Moore. The two would become the leading British avant-garde sculptors of their generation. In 1936 she married Ben Nicholson and in 1939, a week before the outbreak of war, they moved to St Ives in Cornwall, where many artists later settled.

Hepworth's work of the mid-1930s onwards contains only the most oblique reference to the human form but in the late 1940s she reintroduced figurative references: Dyad is one of her most overtly figurative sculptures. On one side there is the incised profile of a man's head and on the other there is a smaller, female profile. The form suggests that the two figures are embracing. There is no front or back view: both sides are equal. Commenting on the title of this work, Hepworth wrote that Dyad was a mathematical term meaning two: 'I used it in this sense of the two forms and the two entities'.

Henry Moore 1898–1986 · *Reclining Figure* 1951

In 1951 London hosted the Festival of Britain exhibition, an event intended to highlight contemporary British art and design and commemorate the centenary of the great Crystal Palace exhibition. The Arts Council of Great Britain commissioned a number of artists to make works for the exhibition. Moore was asked to make a carving of a family group symbolising 'Discovery', but he chose instead to make a large reclining figure in bronze. The Gallery's bronze is this original cast.

Moore later wrote: 'The "Festival Reclining Figure" is perhaps my first sculpture where the space and the form are completely dependent on and inseparable from each other, I had reached the stage where I wanted my sculpture to be truly three-dimensional. In my earlier use of holes in sculpture, the holes were features in themselves. Now the space and form are so naturally fused that they are one.' Moore explained his liking for reclining figures in typically rational terms, observing that large standing figures have a weak point at the ankles. He began making reclining figures in the late 1920s, and in the late 1930s produced several small, bronze reclining figures: these established the long, sinewy form which culminated in this sculpture.

Bronze, 106 × 228.6 × 73.7
Presented by the Arts Council of Great Britain
through the Scottish Arts Council 1969
GMA 1098

Pablo Picasso 1881–1973 · *The Soles (Les Soles)* 1940

Oil on canvas, 60 × 92
Purchased 1967
GMA 1070

On 3 September 1939, two days after the invasion of Poland, Britain and France declared war on Germany. A day earlier Picasso had left Paris for the town of Royan, north of Bordeaux on the Atlantic coast, where he remained based until the following summer. Despite its fish-market subject matter, *The Soles* was painted during a return trip to Paris, where Picasso stayed from March to May (the painting is dated 29 March 1940). In April 1940 Picasso wrote: 'I have done three still lifes with fish, weighing scales, a big crab and eels. In short I am homesick for Royan's marketplace.' The Gallery's painting has traditionally been called *The Soles* but the fish in the scales on the left is not a sole and the crab is perhaps the most dominant element in the composition.

Following the outbreak of the Spanish Civil War, the German bombing of Guernica in 1937, and the declaration of war with Germany,

Picasso's work took on a distinctly aggressive feel. In the early 1940s he made a number of still lifes of animal skulls, skinned sheep's heads and skewered bulls' heads, and food – a precious commodity in occupied Paris – also became a favoured motif. The term 'still life' seems inadequate for such lively works in which the subjects appear to be anything but still.

Pablo Picasso 1881–1973

These drawings formerly belonged to Roland Penrose (see p.124) and were purchased by the Gallery from his estate. Picasso closely identified with the mythological minotaur, who was half man, half beast. Like the harlequin figures of Picasso's early work, the minotaur was an outcast, but he was also a being of untamed passion. He first appeared in Picasso's work in the late 1920s and by the mid-1930s had become one of the artist's favourite motifs, engaged in scenes that were in turns lusty and tragic. Soon after Picasso made the earlier pencil drawing, his friend Paul Eluard wrote a poem about it, noting, 'You have to see yourself die in order to know that you are still alive' – a reference to the mirror held by the woman. The subject of death occurs repeatedly in Picasso's work of this period, when the Civil War was raging in Spain.

The later drawing is a satirical self-portrait of the aged Picasso (who was eighty-six-years old at the time) and his naked model. Sitting on a chamberpot, as if incontinent, he points his phallic pipe in her direction.

Man and Woman (Homme et femme) 1967
Pastel, coloured crayon and wash on paper,
55.6 × 75.2
GMA 3892
Purchased with assistance from the Heritage Lottery
Fund and the National Art Collections Fund 1995
GMA 3892

Death of a Monster (La Fin d'un monstre)
1937
Pencil on paper, 38.6 × 56.3
Purchased with assistance from the Heritage Lottery
Fund and the National Art Collections Fund 1995
GMA 3891

Henri Matisse 1869–1954 · *Jazz* 1947

In 1941 Matisse underwent surgery for cancer, and for much of the remainder of his life he was confined to his bed or wheelchair and could only paint with difficulty. Because of this, many of his late works were made with coloured paper which he simply cut with scissors and pasted onto another sheet. Matisse had used cut paper in several works of the 1930s, notably in cover designs for the art magazines *Cahiers d'Art* and *Verve*. In 1942, Elf Tériade, the publisher of *Verve*, commissioned Matisse to make a whole book of colour images. Matisse began work on the project in 1943, initially conceiving it as a book on the circus. Having made several images on that theme, he then began to select other subjects and motifs. The twenty cut-outs were finished in 1946 and given the title *Jazz*, a name chosen to suggest the exuberance and rhythm of the images. At a late stage Matisse decided to write an accompanying text which was printed in facsimile form: this served to create breathing spaces between the vibrantly coloured images. Matisse compared the structure of text and image in the book to greenery and flowers in a bouquet, the one setting off the other. The text offers a series of loosely connected thoughts on painting, life and the making of the book.

The cut-outs were made into stencils and printed using the same colours Matisse had used in preparing the original pieces of paper. The book was published in September 1947 in an edition of 270 copies with text and 100 copies of the images alone. Three of the page-spreads are illustrated here.

Portfolio with twenty pochoir plates and text,
42 × 65.5 (open page size)
Purchased 1981
GMA 2284

Pablo Picasso 1881–1973 with Pierre Reverdy 1889–1960
The Song of the Dead (Le Chant des morts) 1948

The Gallery has an outstanding
collection of twentieth-century artists'
books, thanks largely to Gabrielle
Keiller's bequest of her art collection
and library in 1995 and to the acquisition the previous year of Roland
Penrose's library and archive. Penrose
(see p.124) was an artist, critic and
writer, and a close friend of Picasso
and many of the Surrealists. This copy
of Le Chant des Morts, comes from the
Penrose library and bears an original
drawing by Picasso on the first page.

Like Matisse's Jazz (see opposite),
Le Chant des Morts was commissioned
and published by Elf Tériade. The
poems, by Pierre Reverdy, were
finished early in 1945 and deal with the
author's wartime experiences in
occupied France. Picasso initially
planned to intersperse the text with
full-page illustrations, but then put the
project aside for two years. After
seeing a medieval manuscript, he
decided to print red brush drawings
directly over Reverdy's handwritten
pages, in the manner of illuminated
manuscripts. The book was issued in
an edition of 270 copies. Two of the
page-spreads are illustrated here.

Book with 125 lithographs and text, 42.5 × 65
(open page size)
Purchased with assistance from the National
Heritage Memorial Fund and the National Art
Collections Fund 1994
GMA A35.L1.11

Fernand Léger 1881–1955 · Tree Trunk on Yellow Ground (Le Tronc d'arbre sur fond jaune) 1945

Léger visited the USA on three separate occasions in the 1930s, and in 1940 took refuge there, as did other prominent European artists including Chagall, Ernst, Duchamp and Mondrian. He was excited by the dynamism, vitality and modernity of America, writing: 'It's a big, tall, wide, limitless place. There is no framework to anything, hundreds of nationalities with as many languages are jumbled up, living jostled together.'

In 1943 Léger went to Montreal where an exhibition of his work had been organised, and on the way chanced upon an abandoned farm at Rousses Point, close to the Canadian border. He was struck by the broken machinery and junk heaped up in the fields and returned there in the summers of 1944 and 1945 with the express intention of painting these various motifs. The circular device on the left is an old wheel with broken spokes, which stands next to a broken 'SLOW' road-sign. Wire netting lies strewn about on the ground. One of the spokes has transformed the road-sign into what can now be read as 'US LOVE'. Referring to the Rousses Point series, Léger later commented: 'The Americans prefer to let agricultural machines go to ruin: three days later they have a new one … So discovering this gave me ideas … Plants grow up around it, birds perch inside it: it all creates marvellous contrasts … '

Oil on canvas, 112.5 × 127
Purchased 1981
GMA 2310

Fernand Léger 1881–1955 · Study for 'The Constructors': the Team at Rest (Etude pour 'Les Constructeurs': l'équipe au repos) 1950

In 1950 Léger made a series of paintings depicting construction workers: these seem to refer to two separate experiences. While out driving near his home west of Paris, he had seen a group of electricians working on some pylons: 'These pylons for high-tension cables were being built along the road. I was struck by the contrast between them, the metallic architecture, which surrounded them and the clouds above.' Elsewhere he referred to ' … a factory being built in the fields. I saw the men balancing high up on the scaffolding.' In some of the paintings the men are shown perched on girders while in others Léger focused on individual workers. The final version, some three metres tall, is in the Léger Museum in Biot, in the south of France.

In 1945 Léger joined the French Communist Party which enjoyed widespread support in France in the late 1940s and early 1950s (Picasso had joined the Party the previous year). From then on, working-class men and women, at work or play, featured in many of his paintings. At the same time his figure drawing became almost neo-classical in inspiration. In 1950 Léger acknowledged that abstract art was on the decline: 'We are witnessing a return to the broad subject which must be comprehensible to the people'. Eager that his art should be seen by ordinary workers, Léger exhibited the series of *Constructors* paintings in the canteen of the Renault car factory in Paris.

Oil on canvas, 162 × 129.5
Purchased 1984
GMA 2845

Balthus b.1908 · *Getting Up (Le Lever)* 1955

Balthasar Klossowski de Rola (he later shortened his name to Balthus) was born in Paris. His father came from an aristocratic Polish family and both parents were painters. Following their separation, Balthus spent the war years with his mother in Berlin and Geneva before returning to Paris in 1924.

By 1930 he was painting works which conjure up a world of sexual awakening poised between the erotic and the sinister. Many of these works feature pubescent girls in suggestive poses, asleep and vulnerable but at the same time apparently conscious of their sexual power. This mood of suppressed eroticism relates to Surrealism, though Balthus was never part of the official group, and his formal means owe as much to Italian Renaissance painting (especially Piero della Francesca) as to French art of the period. His work is maverick compared to that of his contemporaries and his sources were similarly unconventional: nursery rhymes – aimed at children but often carrying mischievous, sinister undertones – were an important influence.

Balthus moved to a château near Nevers, in central France, in 1953 and painted *Getting Up* there. The model was Frédérique Tison, his niece by marriage. Seventeen years old at the time, she became the artist's favourite model and muse. The pose, which derives from paintings by Caravaggio and Corregio, presents a figure at once vulnerable and confrontational.

Oil on canvas, 161 × 130.4
Purchased 1981
GMA 2311

Francis Bacon 1909–92 · *Figure Study I* 1945–46

Bacon was born in Dublin and in the late 1920s spent time in Berlin and Paris before settling in London. It was only after seeing an exhibition of Picasso's work in Paris that he decided to become a painter. Self-taught, he gained some success as a designer of furniture and rugs, but painted comparatively little in the 1930s. He also destroyed much of his work of that period, so very few early paintings survive.

Bacon said that painting only became really important to him in about 1945, the date that his triptych of the previous year, *Three Studies for Figures at the Base of a Crucifixion* (Tate Gallery, London) was exhibited in London. The work was a *succès de scandale* and served to launch the artist's career. Compared to the implicit violence of that work, which depicts three twisted, screaming figures, *Figure Study I* is almost pastoral in feel. It is one of the few works in Bacon's oeuvre which does not feature a figure, though a human presence is suggested under the coat and hat and is made explicit in the title. The painting was followed by a similar work, *Figure Study II* (Huddersfield Art Gallery), which shows the same coat motif, from which a deformed, screaming figure – perhaps lurking under the coat in our painting – emerges. While *Figure Study I* may show the influence of Bacon's close friend Graham Sutherland, it also marks the shift towards a more enigmatic kind of painting, based on the tormented human figure set in the centre of a stage-like space.

Oil on canvas, 123 × 105.5
Accepted by H.M. Government in lieu of Inheritance Tax (Gabrielle Keiller Collection) and allocated to the Scottish National Gallery of Modern Art 1998
GMA 3951

Marino Marini 1901–80 · Pomona 1949

Marini was born in Pistoia. He lived in Florence from 1926 to 1929, then moved to Monza where he taught until 1940. After the war he settled in Milan. His work is strongly indebted to classical Greek, Etruscan and Roman sources. In the 1940s he executed a series of sculptures, prints and drawings of Pomona, the Roman goddess of fruit who watched over the orchards. Normally her attribute is an apple carried in the hand, but here she wears a watch, a ring and a bracelet. The outline of a swimsuit is suggested in places, particularly around the hips and on the back; she may even be wearing a bathing-cap, which would account for her bald head.

Marini visited Paris frequently in the 1930s and certainly saw, and was influenced by, Aristide Maillol's work (see p.22). One of Maillol's most famous sculptures was a Pomona, first made in 1910 and produced in several variants in the 1920s and 1930s. Marini's Pomona may be seen as a light-hearted riposte to the solemn gravity of Maillol's figures.

Bronze, 170 × 80.5 × 58
Presented by Lady Hay 1978
GMA 2027

Germaine Richier 1904–59 · The Runner (Le Coureur) 1955

Bronze, 120 × 59 × 47
Purchased 1974
GMA 1315

Richier studied sculpture under Emile-Antoine Bourdelle (see p.23). During the early 1940s, when she was living in Zurich, she began to blend aspects of the human form with those of insects and even plants. Like Giacometti's postwar work, Richier's was heavily scarred, suggesting decay and anxiety. This emphasis on decomposition and on the solitary, anguished figure was shared with many other artists and writers working in postwar Paris: it contrasts sharply with the full, ripe forms of Maillol's work (see p.22), which typifies French sculpture of the 1920s and 1930s. The emergence of this 'Existentialist' movement in the 1940s has much to do with reactions to the trauma of war. Richier was the leading French sculptor of this postwar period and was as influential in France as Henry Moore was in Britain.

The Runner was originally conceived as a monument for a French sports stadium: there is also a much larger version.

Jean Dubuffet 1901–85 · *Villa by the Road (Villa sur la route)* 1957

Oil on canvas,
81.3 × 100.3
Purchased 1963
GMA 830

Dubuffet studied art for several months in Paris but by 1925 had returned to his home town of Le Havre to work in his father's wine business. In 1930 he moved back to Paris, setting up on his own as a wine merchant. He only painted full-time from 1942. By this date he was working in a deliberately naïve style, influenced by the art of children and the mentally ill. In the late 1940s he began advocating what he called 'Art brut' (Uncultured Art), a movement that has had a profound effect on art since the 1950s.

Owing to the ill health of Dubuffet's wife, from 1955 to 1961 the couple spent much time in Vence, in the south of France. Between April and August 1957 Dubuffet painted twenty-four works in and around Vence: this is one of the earliest of the series.

Wishing to counter traditional art practices, Dubuffet would paint in thick layers, then scratch into the surface to produce a kind of graffiti. Referring to this series, Dubuffet wrote: 'For a very long time I have been attracted by the idea of composing large finished pictures using only the most inadequate means, the way people who have had no training at all draw, like the careless scribblings on barracks walls, seeking an equivalent way of painting, just as rude, just as free from the methods of professional artists. I feel that the elements thus depicted acquire, or might acquire … a much greater dynamic power.'

Giorgio Morandi 1890–1964 · Still Life (Natura Morta) 1962

Morandi was born in Bologna, where he lived for most of his life. He was briefly involved with the Futurist group and, around 1918–19, painted in the 'Metaphysical' style of Giorgio de Chirico and Carlo Carrá, placing apparently unconnected objects such as mannequin heads, bottles and balls together in enigmatic arrangements. He soon abandoned the contrived oddity of these works for still lifes which feature the simplest and most ordinary objects, particularly bottles, jugs and pots. Together with landscape painting, his subject matter and approach hardly changed from the early 1920s until his death in 1964.

Morandi employed a narrow spectrum of colours – mainly dull browns, greens, greys and yellows – and painted in a deliberate, slightly awkward manner, not unlike the Douanier Rousseau, who was one of his favourite artists. Here, the objects are grouped together in the centre of the composition, as if in self-protection, and are painted with a nervous, quivering line. Although Morandi is dealing primarily with shape, space and colour, and seems to avoid all hint of symbolism or narrative, his choice of subject matter and manner of presentation nevertheless suggest qualities of modesty, reflection and silence.

Oil on canvas, 30.5 × 30.6
Purchased 1965
GMA 906

Jackson Pollock 1912–56

Born in Wyoming, Pollock trained under the American regionalist artist Thomas Hart-Benton; other early influences included El Greco, the Mexican mural painters Rivera and Siqueiros, and Picasso and the Surrealists. A severe alcoholic with emotional difficulties, Pollock underwent psychoanalysis between 1937 and 1943, producing drawings as part of his therapy. The probing of the unconscious, his fascination with Jungian psychology, and the technique of automatism advocated by the Surrealists (many of whom moved to New York during the war), all shaped the development of his work. He said, 'When I am painting I am not much aware of what is taking place – it is only after that I see what I have done.' Abandoning traditional methods of composition, draughtsmanship and technique (he often preferred to drip paint with the aid of sticks or a basting syringe), he developed what became known as an 'all-over' manner, avoiding a compositional focus. Pollock became the most celebrated of the American Abstract Expressionists. He was seen as an archetypal American painter – the first American to have forged a new style – and, partly because of him, after the war the centre of interest in the art world shifted from Paris to New York.

The earlier of our two drawings, dating from c.1946, has figurative references, with a human figure drawn in black ink overlaid by what is possibly an animal. The large black drawing is a near duplicate of another. Pollock placed two sheets of thin rice-paper on top of one another and dripped black and red ink onto the first so that much of it bled through to this second sheet; he then added touches of white gouache. The two drawings were probably done on 16 January 1951 at a birthday party for the artist's friend, chief supporter and great champion of Abstract Expressionism, the critic Clement Greenberg. Pollock gave the other version to Greenberg.

Untitled 1951
Ink and gouache on paper, 63.1 × 99.9
Purchased 1963
GMA 849

Untitled c.1946
Oil, pen and ink and watercolour on paper, 50.7 × 33.5
Purchased 1980
GMA 2198

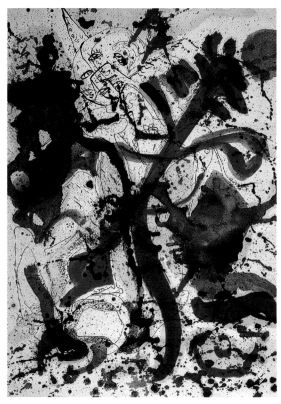

William Gear 1915–97 · *Landscape* 1949

Oil on canvas, 73.5 × 92.5
Purchased 1974
GMA 1300

Gear was born in Methil, Fife, and attended Edinburgh College of Art; he then studied briefly under Fernand Léger in Paris. After the war he worked in Germany, then from 1948 to 1950 lived in Paris where he became affiliated to the Cobra movement. The Cobra artists (the initials stand for Copenhagen, Brussels and Amsterdam, the home cities of many of the group's members), advocated a gestural, near abstract style of painting, influenced by primitivism and the art of children. Gear later remarked of the postwar situation in painting: 'There were no real threads to pick up and start again. The situation was wide open.' The Cobra group was formed at the end of 1948 and Gear showed in their first major exhibition in Amsterdam in November 1949, not long after *Landscape* was painted. Gear thus ranks among the first British artists to work in the gestural, painterly abstract style which would dominate European art in the 1950s.

Although apparently abstract, Gear's works are based on landscape or interior motifs. In *Landscape*, plant-like forms emerge out of a web of black lines in a way suggestive of organic growth.

Nicolas de Staël 1914–55 · The Boat (Le Bateau) 1954

De Staël was born in St Petersburg. The Revolution caused the family to leave Russia and settle first in Poland, then Brussels, where Nicolas studied art. He moved to Paris in 1938, studying briefly under Léger. His work of the 1940s was abstract (the Gallery owns a large oil of 1946), and composed of tangled webs of lines layered over each other. By the early 1950s he was reasserting the importance of subject matter. He bought a house in the south of France in 1953 and from there made regular trips to nearby Marseille, where he made a number of paintings of boats. He abandoned the palette knife and heavy impasto of his earlier work for much thinner, translucent paint which he applied with brushes. The Boat was probably made on a painting trip de

Staël made to the north coast of France, around Calais and Dunkirk in the summer of 1954.

Oil on canvas, 46.3 × 61
Purchased 1962
GMA 817

Oil on canvas, 68.8 × 149
Purchased 1983
GMA 2759

Spencer was born at Cookham in
Berkshire. From 1908 to 1912 he
studied at the Slade School of Art in
London, where contemporaries
included William Roberts, Paul Nash
and Ben Nicholson. He developed his
unusual style very quickly and was
successful from an early age. While
still at the Slade he began his celebrated series of Biblical scenes re-
enacted in the streets of Cookham:
fellow students even nicknamed him
'Cookham'.

From 1945 to 1950 he made a series
of paintings of the Resurrection,
staged in Port Glasgow, where he had
worked as a War Artist; *Christ Delivered
to the People* was painted immediately
afterwards. Pontius Pilate is seen on
the left, washing his hands, while
Christ is led away; the disciples have
turned their backs on Him and scuttle
off in a group.

The year 1950 was a difficult one for
Spencer. Seeking reconciliation with
his first wife, Hilda, he had taken out
divorce proceedings against his
second wife, Patricia Preece. Preece
contested the divorce and, tragically,

Hilda died later that year. The hysteri-
cal woman on the right is probably
Preece. To add to his troubles Spencer
had been threatened with legal action
by Sir Alfred Munnings (a past
President of the Royal Academy), who
declared some of his drawings to be
obscene. The figure tugging at Christ's
sleeve holds a paper which may be
identified with the legal writ issued by
Munnings.

L.S. Lowry 1887–1976 · *Canal and Factories* 1955

Lawrence Stephen Lowry was born in Manchester. He studied art at evening classes but, like his father, made his living as a rent collector and clerk for a firm of accountants (he retired as chief cashier in 1952). An eccentric and reclusive figure, he lived alone after the death of his mother, never travelling and following a spartan, routine existence.

Lowry's art focuses on the industrial cityscapes of Manchester and nearby Salford, affectionately portraying the factories, chimneys and 'matchstick' people who stride purposefully about their business. They are composite 'visions', as Lowry called them, bringing together observed and invented elements drawn from a number of sources. The scene depicted in *Canal and Factories* is based on cityscapes at Runcorn and Widnes, on the river Mersey.

Lowry would invariably paint on a white ground and develop the composition as he went along. Although his paintings may at first seem naïve, they are rigorously composed and intricately patterned, with, for example, the two chimneys on the building in the foreground echoing the two industrial chimneys behind, and the arched roof of the church rhyming wittily with the lamppost beside it and the domed roof on the horizon. The narrow range of tones evokes what Lowry called the 'apocalypse of grime'.

Oil on canvas, 61 × 76.3. Purchased 1975
GMA 1349

Robert MacBryde 1913–66 · *Still Life* c.1947

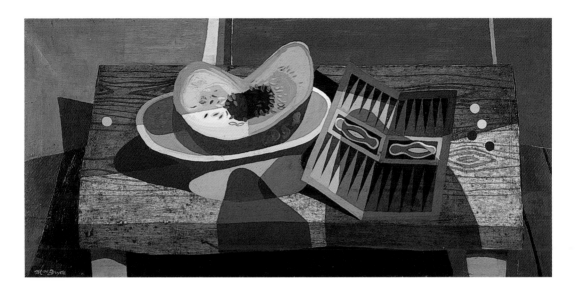

Oil on canvas, 41.5 × 87
Bequeathed by Miss
Elizabeth Watt 1989
GMA 3497

MacBryde's life and career are inextricably linked with Robert Colquhoun (see opposite). Born in Maybole in Ayrshire, MacBryde met Colquhoun at Glasgow School of Art. MacBryde had the more dominant personality and the more highly-strung temperament but he is usually regarded as the less imaginative of the two artists. His works are generally smaller than Colquhoun's and are mainly still lifes. Although MacBryde preferred basic still life arrangements, the objects he selected were often unusual ones, charged with symbolism: phallic cucumbers cut in half appear in many of his pictures. In this *Still Life*, MacBryde presents the unusual combination of a melon – round and feminine in shape – with the aggressively spiked patterns of a backgammon board. This peculiar conjunction of opposites owes something to Surrealism, while the style is derived from Cubism. Two enigmatic shadows cast over the table add a further disturbing note.

Robert Colquhoun 1914–62 · *Figures in a Farmyard* 1953

Colquhoun was born in Kilmarnock. He studied at Glasgow School of Art where he met Robert MacBryde (see opposite). The two immediately formed a close friendship and became known as 'the two Roberts'. For a short time they studied under James Cowie (see p.114) at Hospitalfield House art school, near Arbroath. In 1941 they moved to London where they were drawn into the Neo-Romantic group, finding a studio which they shared with the painter John Minton.

By the mid-1940s Colquhoun had taken the romance out of Neo-Romanticism and had opted for a bleaker, almost existential view of the world. His sharp, aggressive forms seem to reflect what was at times a highly-strung, volatile temperament; and his famously boisterous lifestyle earned him a reputation which threatened to eclipse his art.

Figures in a Farmyard is probably Colquhoun's largest work. Painted when he was living at a cottage near Dunmow in Essex, close to a farm, the figures represent the farmer and his wife. In 1953 Colquhoun was designing costumes for a new production of *King Lear*: the flattened, stage-set forms in this painting may owe something to that project.

Oil on canvas,
185.4 × 143.5
Purchased 1974
GMA 1306

Lynn Chadwick b.1914 · *Winged Figures* 1955

Like Reg Butler (see opposite), Chadwick trained as an architect. During the war he qualified as a pilot, and on demobilisation set up as a textile and furniture designer. His first sculptures were mobiles close in spirit to those of Calder (see p.82). In the early 1950s he embarked upon a series of winged figures which were half-man, half-insect: the wings, like the mobile components in his earlier works, relate to his experience as a pilot.

Although the male and female figures in this sculpture are bonded at the waist in an overtly sexual manner, they belong to a series inspired by rock-and-roll dancing (several similar works by Chadwick are titled *Teddy Boy and Girl*). A year or two later Chadwick made a series of works relating obliquely to the Russian sputnik space programme – like rock-and-roll, a new and decidedly post-war subject.

Chadwick's method of making sculptures has analogies with construction work. He would make an armature with welded iron, then fill the gaps with a mixture of gypsum and iron filings (our sculpture is a bronze cast of the original iron version). *Winged Figures* is a maquette for a much larger work, over two metres tall, now in the Musées Royaux des Beaux-Arts, Brussels.

Bronze,
55.9 × 33.5 × 30.5
Purchased 1960
GMA 761

Reg Butler 1913–81 · Girl 1957–58

Butler trained as an architect but during the war was a conscientious objector and worked as a blacksmith. In the late 1930s and during the 1940s he made a few carvings, but in 1948 began making sculpture from forged and welded iron. This practice, pioneered by Julio González (see p.37), relates to Butler's work as a blacksmith and also to his training in architecture.

Like other British sculptors of the postwar period, Butler felt that the romantic, nature-based imagery of Moore and Hepworth was no longer tenable; sculpture had instead to respond to the collective neuroses of the nuclear age. As he remarked, 'Belsen, Buchenwald, Hiroshima and Nagasaki, were very much in our minds'. In the early 1950s Butler moved away from forged work to modelled figures cast in bronze. Many of his sculptures of these years depict girls. The architectural stand featured in this sculpture derives from Butler's earlier forged metal pieces, but it may also be compared to contemporary works by Bacon and Giacometti in which a cage device serves to hold the figure in empty space and thereby accentuate its solitary nature.

Bronze, 177 × 60.5 × 60.5
Purchased 1962
GMA 809

Alan Davie b.1920

The Saint 1948
Oil on paper, 122 × 89
Purchased with assistance
from the Heritage Lottery
Fund and the National Art
Collections Fund 1997
GMA 4110

The Gallery owns a large collection of
Davie's work, including some twenty
paintings and numerous gouaches,
drawings and prints: many of the
works were given to the Gallery by the
artist in 1997.

Davie was born in Grangemouth,
near Edinburgh, in 1920. He studied at
Edinburgh College of Art where John
Maxwell (see p.117) was one of his
tutors. In 1948 he went on a travelling
scholarship which took him to Italy,
where he saw the work of the American Abstract Expressionists on show
that year at the Venice Biennale. The
Saint, painted in Florence that year,
marks a shift away from the style of the
Edinburgh School towards Expressionist brushwork and mysterious,
iconic subject matter.

By the early 1950s Davie had
abandoned any referential subject
matter and had taken the gestural,
painterly manner a step further, often
laying his canvas or board directly on
the floor and attacking it with broad,
powerful brush strokes, as seen in Blue
Triangle Enters. Abandoning traditional
methods of composition, finish or
even subject matter, he sought to free

his art from premeditated decisions and
instead let intuition and the unconscious take over. This approach owes
much to the artist's interest in Zen
Buddhism and there is also an analogy
with jazz (Davie was a professional jazz
saxophonist early on in his career).

In the later 1950s and 1960s his
brushwork became more controlled
and the imagery more legible: mysterious signs and symbols began to appear.
In 1975 Davie acquired a second home
on the Caribbean island of St Lucia and
this brought about a change in his
working pattern: he would make brush
drawings there during the winter
months and paintings, which develop
from the drawings, in England during
the summer. Reflecting this change, the
paintings from the mid-1970s have a
new precision and clarity and are often
set in stage-like interiors. In the 1980s
the layering of symbols became more
dense. Symbols found in sources as
varied as American Indian pottery,
cosmographic maps, ancient
petroglyphs, aboriginal art and even
phrases from academic text books, all
found their way into his work, mingling
in mysterious and magical ways.

opposite page, clockwise

Blue Triangle Enters 1953
Oil on masonite, 153 × 192
Purchased with assistance from the Heritage Lottery
Fund and the National Art Collections Fund 1997
GMA 4111

Il Mago Study No.1 1987
Oil on canvas, 183 × 152
Presented by the artist 1997
GMA 4122

Lush Life 1961
Oil on canvas, 213 × 173
Presented by the artist 1997
GMA 4113

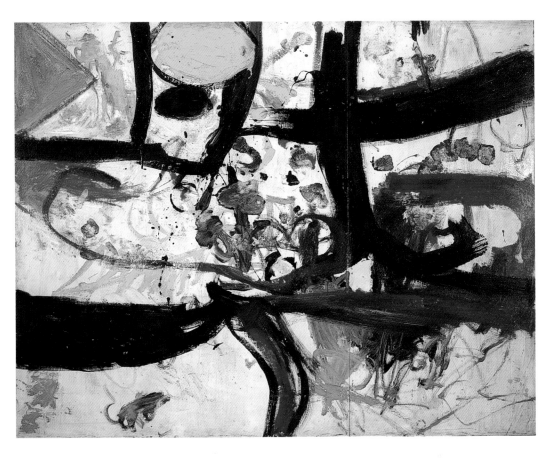

Eduardo Paolozzi b.1924

Growth (or Table Sculpture) 1949
Bronze, 80 × 60.5 × 39
Purchased 1988
GMA 3399

The Gallery has a very large collection of Paolozzi's work. Many important sculptures, collages, drawings and prints were bequeathed in 1995 by Gabrielle Keiller, who had an unrivalled collection of his work. The artist also donated a large number of later works, working studies, prints, and archival material in 1996.

Of Italian descent, Paolozzi was born in Leith near Edinburgh. He lived in Paris from 1947 to 1949 and there produced enigmatic, bronze sculptures which are reminiscent of those of Giacometti. During the same period he made a series of Dada-inspired collages in which magazine advertisements, cartoons and machine parts are combined, thus anticipating the concerns of Pop Art. The interface between popular culture and technology has been a central feature of Paolozzi's art.

He produced comparatively few sculptures until 1956 when he invented an unusual assemblage technique which parallels the collage process. He would press objects such as cogs, nuts and machine parts into clay to leave an imprint, pour wax over the surface, lift the wax off when dry,

and construct sculptures from these wax sheets. The fragile assemblage would then be cast in bronze. The shattered, encrusted figures that emerged from this process seem like survivors of a nuclear holocaust, at once noble, menacing and fragile.

In the 1960s Paolozzi extended the principle of collage and interchangeability by making sculptures which have no fixed order, as in *Domino*. The nine elements can be stacked on top of one another or laid out in any number of permutations. Such an approach is partly indebted to children's toy kits, which have always fascinated the artist. *Master of the Universe* is characteristic of Paolozzi's more recent work in which a plaster model is cut up and reassembled in a slightly dislocated form. It is based on a drawing of Newton by William Blake and is a model for the large bronze outside the new British Library in London.

St Sebastian I 1957
Bronze, 214.5 × 72 × 35.5
Purchased 1993
GMA 3700

Domino 1967–68
Aluminium, tallest element
310 high
Presented by Gabrielle
Keiller 1984
GMA 2826

Master of the Universe
1989
Bronze,
147 × 190.2 × 106.5
Purchased 1990
GMA 3580

Terry Frost b.1915 · *Black and White Movement on Blue and Green II* 1951–52

Oil on canvas, 111.8 × 86.3
Purchased 1974
GMA 1299

Frost was born in Leamington Spa. He began painting when he was a prisoner of war in Germany. He moved to Cornwall in 1946, studying at art school in St Ives. From 1947 to 1950 he studied in London. He returned to St Ives in 1950 and at the time this painting was made was working as an assistant to Barbara Hepworth.

Black and White Movement on Blue and Green II was inspired by the sight of boats moored in St Ives harbour. Commenting on the first version of this painting, Frost said that he was struck by 'what I can only describe as a synthesis of movement and counter-movement. That is to say the rise and fall of the boats, the space drawing of the mast-heads, the opposing movements of the incoming sea and outblowing off-shore wind ... I was not portraying subject matter but concentrating on the emotion engendered by what I saw.' The title underlines the independence of the painting from the initial subject.

The first version of the painting is in the Tate Gallery in London. This is a second, slightly different version.

Peter Lanyon 1918–64 · *Solo Flight* 1960

Lanyon was born in St Ives, Cornwall. He met Nicholson, Hepworth and Gabo, who moved to the St Ives area in 1939, and was encouraged by them. Although Lanyon's work from the late 1940s onwards appears at first to be entirely abstract, its point of reference is the Cornish and West Country landscape. However, instead of showing fidelity to topographic features, Lanyon's main concern was to evoke space and air.

In 1959 he began gliding – an experience which had a profound effect on his later work. He remarked that: '*Solo Flight* was one of the first pictures done after I had learned to glide and fly around the coast. The red is the track of something moving over the surface of the painting, and, at the same time, the track of the aircraft moving over the ground below. Blue air merges with the land. I wanted to get the sense of something far away and down below inside the red track.'

Lanyon described gliding as 'a way to participate in the air around the coast and in this way to experience my county from outside.' He died in 1964 following a gliding accident.

Oil on masonite, 121.5 × 183
Purchased 1983
GMA 2742

Joan Eardley 1921–63

Street Kids c.1949–51
Oil on canvas,
102.9 × 73.7
Purchased with funds given by an anonymous donor
1964
GMA 887

streets. Life is at its most uninhibited here. Dilapidation is often more interesting to a painter as is anything that has been used and looks used … ' *Street Kids* was painted shortly after her return from Italy while *Children and Chalked Wall 3* (one of four versions) was begun in January 1962 and re-worked a year later. The latter depicts two children from the Samson family, who lived locally and feature in many of her paintings. The stencilled lettering and fragments of collaged newspaper imitate graffiti; the silver and gold papers are probably sweet wrappers.

Eardley first visited the fishing village of Catterline, on the east coast, south of Aberdeen, in 1950 and bought a small, very basic cottage there in 1954. From then on she spent most of her time in Catterline. Like Townhead, Catterline was a small, intimate community, where everyone knew one another. She mainly painted the village, harbour and sea, continuing even in the most appalling weather. Some of these works feature collaged grasses and sand. *Catterline in Winter* was painted in January 1963. Her cottage is seen at the far left, though by that time she was using it as a studio and was living in a more comfortable house at the other end of the row. Her work has the freedom of execution one finds in abstract painting (she was an admirer of De Kooning's work in particular) but also carries the emotional weight abstraction sometimes lacks. Here the cottages seem to be bracing themselves for a cold, hard winter; the sun or moon above hardly illuminates the leaden sky.

Eardley died of cancer in August 1963. Her ashes were scattered on the beach at Catterline. The Gallery owns twelve of her paintings and more than 200 drawings, most of them given by the artist's sister, Pat Black.

Eardley was born in Sussex. Her family moved to Glasgow at the outbreak of war. She studied at Glasgow School of Art and, briefly, at Hospitalfield House under James Cowie. In 1949, following a scholarship year spent mainly in Italy, she rented a studio in the centre of Glasgow. She moved to the Townhead area of the city a couple of years later.

Cowie had often painted children (see p.114) and the local street children were to be Eardley's favourite subjects in her Glasgow years. Adult figures rarely appear in her work. She stated: 'I like the friendliness of the back

Children and Chalked Wall 3
1962–63
Oil, newspaper and metal
foil on canvas,
61 × 68.6
Purchased 1963
GMA 853

Catterline in Winter
1963
Oil on hardboard,
120.7 × 130.8
Purchased 1964
GMA 888

Robin Philipson 1916–92 · *Fighting Cocks, Grey c.1961*

Oil on canvas, 63 × 75.8
Purchased 1961
GMA 788

Born at Broughton-in-Furness, Cumbria, Philipson moved with his family to Scotland when he was fourteen. He studied at Edinburgh College of Art from 1936 to 1940, and in 1947 joined the teaching staff. He taught at the College until 1982, when he retired as Head of Drawing and Painting. His early work – mainly landscapes, still lifes and interiors – was strongly influenced by Kokoschka, whose painting *Zrání* (see p.63) Philipson had studied at length. Later in the 1950s he became more interested in the work of the American Abstract Expressionists.

Philipson served in India during the war and among the many sketches he made there was a watercolour of people watching a cock fight. Ten years later, in 1952, he returned to the theme. The earliest of these works include figures around the fighting cocks but he soon began to concentrate on the birds alone. He even went to a poultry research laboratory to study the birds at close quarters. The violent, frenetic movement of the cocks provided the perfect analogue for the free, gestural style which Philipson was then exploring. He remarked: 'It all became a sequence of gestures, abstract relationships of wings to bodies, heads to necks, totally grotesque and out of character, but somehow the speed of it all, and the ferocity, combined with their stateliness ... ' Philipson continued painting cockfights during the 1960s: contemporaneous with these works is a series on a much calmer theme, cathedral rose windows.

John Bellany b.1942 · *Allegory* 1964

Bellany was born in the fishing village of Port Seton, near Edinburgh. His father and both grandfathers were fishermen. He studied at Edinburgh College of Art from 1960 to 1965. In his postgraduate year, in the autumn of 1964, Bellany began painting *Allegory*, his largest and most ambitious work to date. At a time when abstract art was becoming the norm, Bellany made a conscious decision to follow in the footsteps of the Old Masters (particularly those of the northern schools, such as Breughel, Steen and even Wilkie) and make figurative painting grounded in his own experience.

The formal layout of *Allegory* derives from Grünewald's *Isenheim Altarpiece*, but the subject matter is autobiographical. As a student, Bellany had a Saturday job gutting fish in Port Seton. The setting of *Allegory* is a mixture of Port Seton and Eyemouth (where his grandparents lived) while the Bass Rock can be seen on the horizon. The gutted haddock, displayed in the manner of the Crucifixion, become metaphors for suffering humanity; the passive fishermen replace Christ's family and the soldiers. The triptych was exhibited at Bellany's postgraduate exhibition in 1965, when the artist was twenty-three years old.

Oil on hardboard (triptych),
212.4 × 121.8; 213.3 × 160; 212.5 × 121.8
Purchased 1988
GMA 3359

Antoni Tàpies b.1923 · Violet Grey with Wrinkles (Gris violacé aux rides) 1961

Mixed media on canvas,
200 × 176
Purchased 1983
GMA 2760

Tàpies was born in Barcelona where he read law. His early work (he was self-taught) combines influences from Dada, Surrealism and Paul Klee. In the 1950s he began 'painting' with a thick paste made of glue, marble dust, plaster and paint: the substance resembles cement or volcanic lava. He would coat the canvas with it and then draw into the tacky surface, making marks suggestive of stains, scars, wounds and decomposition. Like Dubuffet (see p.142), Tàpies was strongly influenced by the art of the insane and by graffiti, and his work may also be associated with the pessimism of the Existentialist movement. Most of his paintings are black or grey – indeed he blocks the daylight out of the studio in which he works.

The wall has been a continuous motif in Tàpies's work and he has related it to the high walls of the dark, narrow streets of Barcelona and Catalonia where he lives. He remarks: 'The image of the wall can contain countless suggestions. Separation, claustrophobia; wailing walls, prison walls; rejection of the world, contemplation, destruction of passion, silence, death; laceration, torture, torn bodies, human debris ... '

Louise Nevelson 1899–1988 · Nightscape 1957–64

Nevelson was born in Kiev in 1899; the family moved to America five years later. Her father worked in a lumber yard where the young Louise made her first sculptures. She moved to New York in 1920 and lived there for the rest of her life. Influenced partly by Surrealism, partly by Mexican sculpture, she assembled sculptures from scraps of wood in the early 1940s. For an exhibition held in 1955 she abandoned traditional plinths, instead making the stands – constructed from old wooden crates – integral parts of the works: this in turn led to a series of shallow assemblages made from vegetable and bottle crates. The simple expedient of storing them against a wall, stacked one on top of another, led to her celebrated wall assemblages, which date from 1957. In her exhibitions these became total environments which enveloped the spectator. The elements in each were potentially variable, since they were made up of the same basic grammar of boxed elements: units from one wall could be dismantled and incorporated into another – hence the seven-year date span of this work, finished in 1964 but incorporating parts dating back to the 1950s. Most of Nevelson's works were painted black but there are others in white and gold.

Commenting on these works, Nevelson said: 'I see New York City as a great big sculpture ... This is what I have lived in ... towards evening or morning, when the buildings are silhouetted and they are not disturbed by that much activity, you will see that many of my works are real reflections of the city.'

Painted wood and formica assemblage,
258.5 × 347 × 42
Purchased 1980
GMA 2194

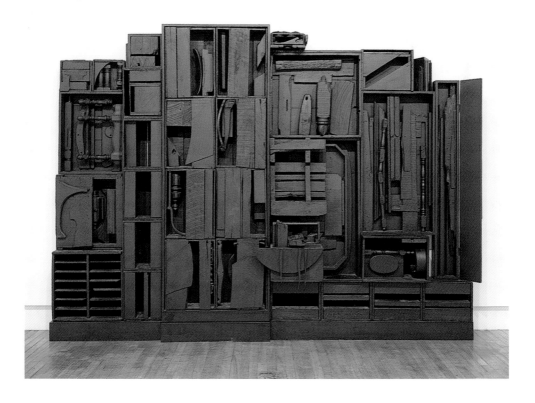

William Turnbull b.1922 · *Night* 1962–63

Turnbull was born in Dundee. He studied at the Slade School of Art in London and, along with a number of British artists of his generation (Gear, Paolozzi, Freud), lived in Paris after the war. He moved back to London in 1950. His work featured alongside that of Butler, Chadwick, Paolozzi and others in the British pavilion at the 1952 Venice Biennale.

Turnbull's works of the late 1940s and early 1950s were in bronze and had worn, crusty surfaces. His bronzes of the mid- to late 1950s were taller and totemic in structure. In about 1959 he chanced upon a load of rosewood logs at a timber merchant's in north London: he bought the lot. Making slight modifications to the wood (he had not previously done any carving)

he produced a series of works in which several elements, often in different materials, are stacked on top of each other. Other works of the period feature stone elements in addition to rosewood and bronze. These works suggest ancient, primitive idols, mysterious things which, in another culture, might be the focus of worship; this is a feeling reinforced in *Night* by the cruciform shape. The sliced ovoid form which sits delicately on the horizontal bar developed from Turnbull's fascination with opening flowers, and was partly inspired by Monet's late water lily paintings; the form also reads as a head gazing upward. Echoing Brancusi's work, the traditional distinction between base and sculpture is eliminated.

Bronze and rosewood,
161.4 × 124.5 × 43
Purchased 1984
GMA 2831

Barbara Hepworth 1903–75 · *Conversation with Magic Stones* 1973

In 1934 Hepworth gave birth to triplets and thereafter made a number of works featuring three main elements. *Conversation with Magic Stones* repeats the forms found in some of the artist's work of the 1930s. It features three tall 'figures' standing over three smaller ones, which the artist referred to as 'magic stones'.

Most of Hepworth's early works were carved in stone or wood (see p.130), and it was only in the 1950s that she took to casting work in metal. As her fame grew, so the advantages of working in bronze (speed, durability and the possibility of making duplicate casts) became more apparent. She did, however, approach bronze with a carver's technique, first making the works in plaster which she carved, cut

and filed prior to casting in bronze. Most of Henry Moore's bronzes are recumbent, horizontal figures, while Hepworth preferred the upright form. Hepworth lived in St Ives, Cornwall, and the many prehistoric dolmens in the area seem to have inspired works such as this.

Bronze, six elements, maximum height 282
Accepted by H.M. Government in lieu of death duties; presented 1978
GMA 2000

Oil and magna on canvas,
172 × 203.5
Purchased 1980
GMA 2133

Lichtenstein was born in New York. Having previously painted in the Abstract Expressionist mode, in 1961 he began making variants of comic-strip cartoons, using the Benday dot technique of magazine reproductions. In common with many Pop artists (the term was in use from 1962), Lichtenstein was reacting against the emotional involvement of Abstract Expressionism and was instead turning to popular, consumer culture – fast-food packaging, comic-strips, magazine advertisements – for inspiration. His work aroused great controversy when it was first exhibited.

In the Car is one of a number of pictures from the early 1960s in which Lichtenstein dealt with the theme of romance – a subject previously shunned by most 'serious' twentieth-century artists. With deliberate irony, he counterpoints the emotional drama of the imagery with the bland, mechanical method of representation. Blown up to such large scale, they become quintessential images of modern America, at once glamorous, mundane, dramatic and impersonal. In common with his other paintings of the period, *In the Car* develops from a comic-strip illustration found in a magazine (*Girls' Romances* was one of his favourite sources). He would make a small drawing after the original, project it onto the bare canvas, then make adjustments to the design.

Andy Warhol 1928–87 · Portrait of Maurice 1976

Warhol worked as a commercial artist in the 1950s and the techniques and imagery he developed during this period fed seamlessly into his paintings of the 1960s. He made his first paintings based on advertisements in 1960. Warhol chose imagery that was ubiquitous and archetypally American: soup cans, coke bottles, dollar bills, film stars. These were the new icons of post-war consumer culture. Whereas Lichtenstein used Benday dots, Warhol used the equally anonymous technique of screenprint. His screenprinting often has a smudged, out-of-register look which heightens the sense of artificiality.

One of Warhol's obsessions was fame: he declared that everyone would be famous for fifteen minutes. From the 1970s he made commissioned portraits of pop stars, film stars and the rich, and in the mid-1970s he extended this commercial activity to include people's pets: they too could enjoy a moment of stardom. In Warhol's art, fame, glamour, artifice and banality became blurred, perfectly mirroring the age of mass consumerism. In 1976 he held two exhibitions devoted to his animal pictures. Gabrielle Keiller (who bequeathed her superb collection of modern art to the Gallery in 1995) saw the exhibition *Cats and Dogs* and commissioned a portrait of her beloved dachshund, Maurice. Warhol visited her at her home near London and took the Polaroid photographs which served as the basis for the screenprinted image.

Oil and silk-screen on canvas, 65.8 × 81.4
Bequeathed by Gabrielle Keiller 1995
GMA 4095

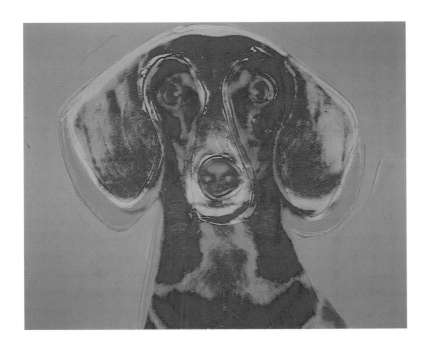

Roger Hilton 1911–75 · Dancing Woman 1963

Hilton was born in Middlesex. His father was of German origin but had the family name, Hildesheim, anglicised during the First World War. From 1957 Hilton spent an increasing proportion of his time in St Ives in Cornwall, settling there in 1965. During this period he moved away from abstraction and began to incorporate landscape and figurative motifs into his work.

Dancing Woman was inspired by an incident which took place in the summer of 1963. Rose Hilton, the artist's wife, recalled: 'In 1963 Roger and I with our 18 month-old son were on holiday in mid France, we were staying for three months in an isolated village. It was left to me to shop at the nearest town, some ten miles away, we

had no transport, and in rebellion, after returning hot and dusty, with the food and drink supplies for a week, I drank some rum, undressed and danced nude on the balcony, not noticing that the firemen and locals were busy putting out a fire in a hay-rick in the fields opposite. Nor did I notice that they had transferred their attention to the balcony.' Hilton remarked of the painting: 'It was my wife dancing on the veranda, we were having a quarrel. She was nude and angry at the time and she was dancing up and down shouting "oi yoi yoi".' The first version, titled Oi Yoi Yoi, is in the Tate Gallery, London. Hilton painted this second version immediately afterwards.

Oil and black chalk on canvas, 152.5 × 127
Purchased 1981
GMA 2463

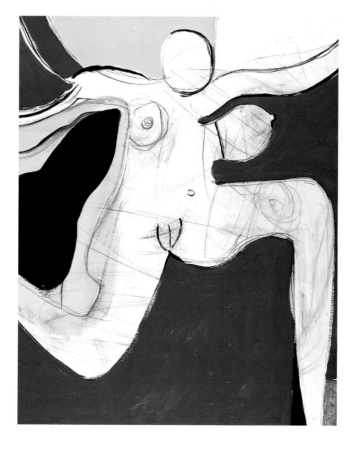

David Hockney b.1937 · *Rocky Mountains and Tired Indians* 1965

Hockney was born in Bradford. He won widespread recognition while still a student at the Royal College of Art in London. He moved to Los Angeles in 1964 and still lives there. *Rocky Mountains and Tired Indians* was painted in the summer of 1965 at the University of Colorado, Boulder, where the artist held a six-week teaching post. Hockney commented that it was 'an attractive campus on the edge of the Rocky Mountains ... I was given a studio that had no window to look out of, no windows to view the Rocky Mountains ... So I painted *Rocky Mountains and Tired Indians*. The whole picture is an invention from geological magazines and romantic ideas (the nearest Indians are at least three hundred miles from Boulder).' The striped mountains in the background were a light-hearted response to contemporary striped, abstract paintings by American artists such as

Kenneth Noland and Morris Louis. Hockney remarked: 'The chair was just put in for compositional purposes, and to explain its being there I called the Indians "tired".' The Indians and the totem pole were painted from photographs.

Acrylic on canvas,
170.4 × 252.8
Purchased 1976
GMA 1538

Jean Tinguely 1925–91 · *Blind Jealousy II (La Jalousie II)* 1961

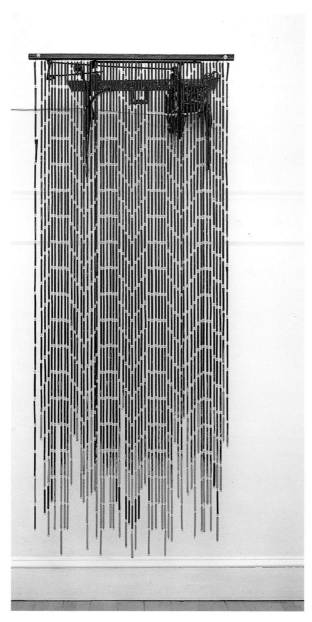

Tinguely was born in Switzerland. In 1953 he moved to Paris. He was one of a number of artists of the period exploring movement or Kinetic art. In the mid-1950s he made complicated but seemingly fragile sculptures from wire: they moved and made clanking noises when a crank was turned or a motor switched on. One series of mechanical sculptures, begun in the late 1950s, incorporates pens which jiggle up and down, creating abstract drawings. These works were ironic comments on the fashion for gestural, action painting.

Tinguely was one of a number of mainly French artists belonging to the *Nouveaux Réalistes* (New Realists) group, which was founded in 1960 and whose members worked with urban junk rather than with traditional artists' materials. César and Arman (see opposite and p.174) were also part of the group. For them, as for the Pop Artists, waste material said more about contemporary society than paint or bronze ever could. Tinguely was particularly interested in undermining the idea that machines were a positive, rational force in society. When the electric button on *La Jalousie* is pressed, the bead curtain jumps into action, swaying furiously but also sensuously, much like the grass skirt of an exotic dancer. The title is an untranslatable pun on the French word 'jalousie', which means both jealousy and a blind or bead curtain.

Painted bead curtain, metal rod and electric motor,
217.5 × 91.5 × 35.5
Purchased 1984
GMA 2832

César 1921–98 · *Compression* 1966

César (like Arman he uses an abridged form of his name) was born in Marseille. His early work was made from soldered and welded metal, and bears comparison with contemporary work by British sculptors such as Chadwick and Paolozzi (see pp.152 and 156–157). By 1960 César was considered one of France's leading sculptors.

In May 1960 César astonished his followers by apparently changing direction and showing three crushed cars at a Paris exhibition. On one of his regular forays in search of metal, César had visited a scrap merchant and seen a newly installed hydraulic crushing machine in operation. He said that when he saw the machine for the first time 'I was completely struck by it and immediately wanted to use it myself.' He was also conscious that the massive stacks of scrap metal made small-scale welded sculptures seem trifling by comparison. He selected particular cars for crushing, mixing elements from differently coloured vehicles and inserting them at carefully judged angles: in this way he gained some control over the surface pattern and colour scheme. The 'Renault' nameplate is prominent on the present work. Like Arman and Tinguely (see p.174 and opposite), César was part of the French New Realism movement which found its inspiration in urban life.

Compressed automobile parts, 162 × 68.5 × 66
Purchased 1982
GMA 2505

Arman b.1928 · Cello in Space (Violoncelle dans l'espace) 1967–68

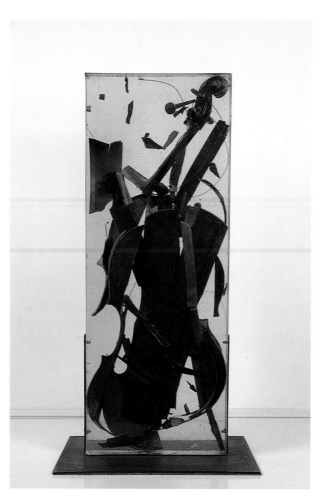

Fragmented cello in polyester resin,
127.9 × 48.6 × 14.6
Purchased 1983
GMA 2793

Arman was born in Nice. He moved to Paris in 1949 and since the early 1960s has lived in New York. Although his full name was Armand Fernandez, early in his career a catalogue misprint reduced his name to Arman, and he has worked under that name ever since.

In the 1950s he made works on paper covered with the imprints of inked-up rubber stamps. These repeated patterns led, in 1959, to his *Accumulations*, in which real objects are crammed into transparent plastic boxes. The boxes contain dozens of identical, manufactured items: gas masks, telephones, dolls, lightbulbs, used envelopes. At the same time, Arman was a pioneer of the Happening, an artform which evolved in the late 1950s and early 1960s, and which, in his case, involved smashing up pianos, cars, even whole rooms. At first he fixed the broken remains onto panels but, from 1962, took to setting them in clear polyester resin: he called the series *Colère* (Anger). The approach is not unlike Pollock's Action Painting (see pp.144–145) transposed to a three dimensional medium, and there are also parallels with the boxed art of Schwitters, Duchamp and Cornell (see pp.58, 66 and 85). This work was made by pouring resin into a flat box, to the depth of about a centimetre, and inserting elements of the cello; once set, another layer of resin could be poured, and more of the pieces added. The final work is like a cello frozen in space a fraction of a second after it has exploded.

Günter Brus b.1938 · Untitled (Ohne Titel) 1965

*Mixed media on board
mounted on wood, 77 × 77
Purchased 1987
GMA 3054*

Brus was part of the Viennese Action Group (Wiener Aktionsgruppe), which emerged in the early 1960s. Their art developed from – but was also a critique of – the Action Painting of Jackson Pollock (see pp.144–145), which in Europe in the 1950s had been popularised in a type of painting known as *Informel* and *Tachisme*. By 1960 that type of painting – abstract, gestural mark-making – had become formulaic and orthodox, and the early 1960s saw a general return to figuration in, for example, the art of Lichtenstein, Warhol and Baselitz.

Brus and the Viennese action artists (who included Otto Mühl, Hermann Nitsch and, later, Rudolf Schwarzkogler) wanted to present the actions inherent in Action Painting as directly as possible, and not as traces of paint on canvas. Using their bodies as the subject of their work, they did this by actually painting themselves. This work documents a 'Self-painting' Brus did in Vienna at the end of 1964. He began by painting his hands, his head and then his whole body, and finished by painting black lines over himself to suggest cracks tearing through the body. The collaged pins, razor blades and pen-knife take on the ritual significance of tools of torture; the body is like that of a secular saint. By using their bodies in this way, Brus and the action artists were reintroducing raw human emotion into art. Work of this kind is emblematic of the counter-culture which operated throughout Europe and the USA during the 1960s, but this collage also refers to the tortured self-portraits of the Viennese Expressionists, Egon Schiele and Oskar Kokoschka.

Joe Tilson b.1928 · Nine Elements 1963

Born in London, Tilson first worked as a carpenter and joiner. He trained at the Royal College of Art in London in the early 1950s. Later in the decade he produced wood reliefs which are comparable to those of Schwitters (see p.58), before developing his own Pop imagery in the early 1960s.

Nine Elements is part painting, part sculpture. It is a compendium of images, most of which Tilson had previously used as independent paintings; the hot-rod car flames had also appeared in an earlier work. The structure of the work is reminiscent of children's learning games and the juxtapositions of images and styles

invites the viewer to decode or invent a meaning. The images suggest a variety of senses and concepts: touch, sight, sound or taste ('vox' is Latin for voice), hearing (the cipher bottom right is a Miróesque ear), time and chance. The bespectacled eye on a television screen derives from a photograph of Tilson himself. The underlying theme of *Nine Elements*, and of much of Tilson's work of this date, is language and communication and the relationship between words and symbols. The manner of representation varies from naturalistic to televisual to abstract, from the verbal ('vox') to the real (the keyhole) to the conceptual (the question-mark).

Mixed media on wood relief,
259 × 182.8
Purchased 1983
GMA 2761

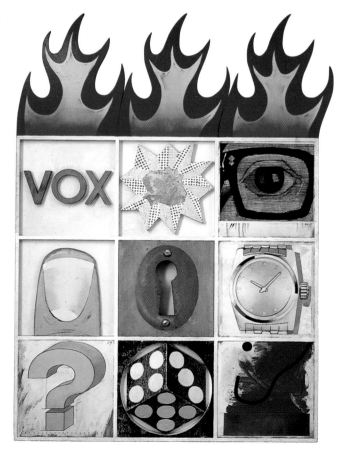

176

Richard Hamilton b.1922 · Desk 1964

Hamilton was born in London. During the 1950s he was an influential figure in the move away from Abstract Expressionism towards a more cerebral, conceptual type of work. His early preoccupation with consumer culture and the imagery of advertising makes him one of the forerunners of Pop Art. He was much indebted to Marcel Duchamp (see pp.66–67), introducing wit, irony and dislocation into his work, and avoiding a particular style. It could even be said that style is the subject of his work. He has used photography, painting, installation and printmaking, often in combination, and always in a questioning, critical way.

In 1964 Hamilton made a number of works based on a publicity photograph for the 1948 B-movie *Shockproof*. *Desk* is a study for an important element in two larger paintings, *Interior I* and *Interior II*. The publicity shot had a strange, distorted perspective and, with its self-consciously modern props, it seemed to suggest a narrative all of its own. The scene features an actress standing in a stage-set, with a desk in the foreground. The woman has just killed a man: in the painting he lies hidden behind the desk but his presence is indicated by the smudged blood on the floor. *Desk* presents a deliberately ambiguous marriage of conflicting styles and meanings. The background is a Mondrianesque tapestry of geometric forms; the blood imitates the brushwork of Abstract Expressionism; and the real and false wood-graining on the desk recall the collage techniques of Cubism. Part descriptive and narrative, part abstract and part photographic, it fuses the machine-made and the painterly.

Oil and collage on photograph, laid on panel, 62.5 × 89
Purchased 1980
GMA 2155

Born in Hungary, Vasarely is known as the father of Op Art. The term, indicating a concern with optical effects (and a distinction from contemporaneous Pop Art), was coined at the time of the exhibition *The Responsive Eye* held at the Museum of Modern Art, New York, in 1965. Art incorporating optical and kinetic effects became very popular in the mid-to-late 1960s, finding its way onto everything from dress designs to record sleeves.

Vasarely moved to Paris in 1930. He worked mainly as a graphic artist and it was not until the 1940s that he returned to painting. He began the geometric abstract works for which he is known in 1947, initially drawing inspiration from the cracked tiles he looked at every day while waiting for the underground train in Paris. His work initially owed much to a preceding generation of east European artists, especially Moholy-Nagy (see p.41) and the Russian Constructivists. Like them, he was idealistic: he wrote numerous manifestos and attacked the cult of individualism (his vast body of work was made mainly by assistants). By the mid-1950s he was producing paintings in which asymmetrical geometric patterns, repeated with varying degrees of frequency and distortion, produce extraordinary optical effects of depth and movement. Vasarely often gave his paintings titles of geographical origin: Taïmyr is the name of a lake and river in the far north of Russia.

Oil on canvas, 162 × 130
Purchased 1973
GMA 1279

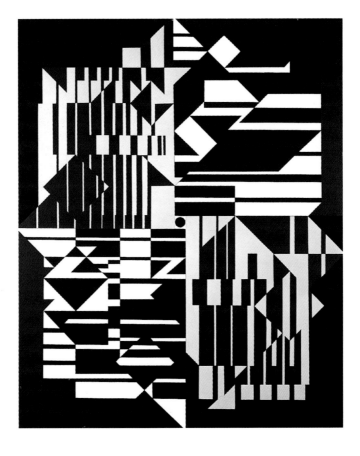

Bridget Riley b.1931 · *Over* 1966

Emulsion on board,
101.5 × 101.3
Purchased 1974
GMA 1316

Riley was born in London. Influenced in particular by the work of Seurat, the Futurists and American colour-field painting, in 1960–61 she made her first experiments with optical movement in painting. Using the same basic units – squares, circles, spirals and lines – subjected to subtle variations in size and progression across the picture plane, she managed to create complex optical sensations of movement, rhythm and energy. For several years she worked exclusively in black and white before introducing greys and colours in the mid-1960s. By that date she had gained an international reputation and her work was widely imitated.

Although abstract, the sensations provoked by Riley's work correspond to sensations we encounter in the natural world: dazzling light, movement, sharp contrasts, compression. Of this painting, Riley remarked: 'The theme of the painting *Over* is a certain sensation of change: moving from one state to another, a transition enacted through the progression of the elements employed. Something crosses "over", turns "over". This is a persistent principle of my work which appears involuntarily in different guises at different times.'

Frank Auerbach b.1931 · *E.O.W. IV* 1961

Born in Berlin, Auerbach left Nazi Germany in 1939, moving to England. After the war he settled in London and in the late 1940s he studied under David Bomberg (see p.109). In 1954 he took over Leon Kossoff's studio in Camden Town (see p.185) and he has used the same studio ever since.

Auerbach has mainly painted landcapes and townscapes in the Camden Town area, and portraits of a few close friends. The numerous portraits of his companion Stella West (always referred to by her inititals, E.O.W.), were done from about 1952 to 1972. Throughout that period she posed for him three evenings a week, always by electric light. Auerbach has commented on these portraits: 'I was living with someone, who has the inititals E.O.W. She was the most important person in my life at the time ... The intensity of life with somebody and the sense of its passing has its own pathos and poignancy. There was a sense of futility about it all disappearing into the void and I just wanted to pin something down that would defy time, so it wouldn't all just go off into thin air.' The very thick paint, which is typical of Auerbach's work, comes from this desire to fix and 'pin down'. The final image is not an accumulation of paint applied over a period of months; instead Auerbach regularly scrapes off all the paint and starts afresh almost daily. For many years he painted largely in monochrome, partly because these paints were cheaper and partly due to the influence of Rembrandt. The Gallery also owns two landscapes by Auerbach.

Lucian Freud b.1922 · *Two Men* 1987–88

Freud was born in Berlin. The family moved to England in 1933. He studied at the Central School of Arts and Crafts in London and then intermittently at the East Anglian School of Painting and Drawing, but was largely self-taught. In the 1940s he became interested in Surrealism, but his works have always been based on a close scrutiny of the real world.

Most of Freud's works are studio portraits or figure compositions. He depicts the same friends, or more usually paid models, over and over again. This painting was completed in July 1988. In between sessions of working on a large, full-length double portrait of the same two men (*Two Men in the Studio*, 1987–89), in which the naked figure is standing, Freud began a painting of his models resting on a mattress on the floor of his studio. He became so absorbed by it that he temporarily put aside the larger painting. The intensity of the artist's gaze meets its opposite in the image of two relaxed figures. As in many of Freud's paintings, the pose is apparently casual but slightly provocative, the clothed man gently resting his hand on the other's calf. The Gallery also owns a number of etchings by Freud.

Oil on canvas, 106.7 × 75
Purchased 1988
GMA 3410

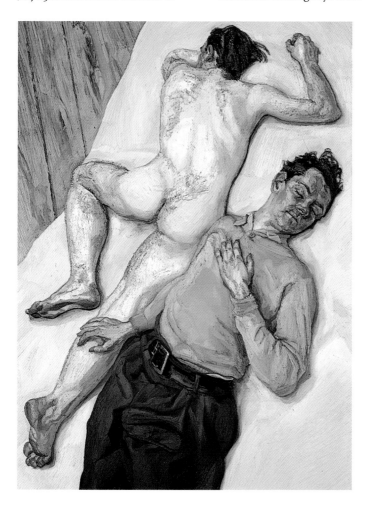

Born in Cleveland, Ohio, Kitaj settled in Britain in 1957; he moved to Los Angeles in 1997. In London in the 1970s he became identified with a loose grouping of artists (Bacon, Freud, Auerbach, Kossoff and Andrews) who were concerned with the human form. The group is now referred to as the School of London.

If Not, Not is probably Kitaj's best-known and most complex work. He has written: 'Two main strands come together in the picture. One is a certain allegiance to T.S. Eliot's *Wasteland* and its (largely unexplained) family of loose assemblage. Eliot used, in his turn, Conrad's *Heart of Darkness*, and the dying figures among the trees to the right of my canvas make similar use of Conrad's bodies strewn along the riverbank.' Eliot is depicted at the bottom left, wearing a hearing aid. The second 'strand' is the holocaust: the building which towers over the landscape is the gatehouse to Auschwitz. Below it lies a scene of cultural disintegration and moral collapse. The stagnant water, the dead and blackened trees, and the books scattered about the landscape, speak of death and destruction. A Matisse bust (by coincidence, a variant of the one owned by the Gallery – see p.25) lies broken in the centre foreground. The small figure of the man in bed, holding a baby, is a self-portrait. There are other references to paintings by Giorgione and Bassano.

A huge tapestry version of the painting was made for the foyer of the new British Library in London in 1996–97.

Oil and black chalk on canvas, 152.4 × 152.4
Purchased 1976
GMA 1585

Andrews is linked with the School of London (Bacon, Freud, Kossoff, Auerbach and Kitaj), although he lived for many years in the Norfolk countryside. He first visited Scotland in 1975 and returned regularly thereafter, making a series of paintings on the theme of deer stalking. *Edinburgh (Old Town)* is his last Scottish painting and one of his last major works. Instead of painting the familiar view of the castle from the north, Andrews shows its more forbidding south-facing aspect. The area is known as the Grassmarket, and it is here that public hangings were held and mob violence erupted. (Such activities are described in Walter Scott's *Heart of Midlothian*, a book which partly inspired the painting.) The site of the gallows is commemorated by a walled enclosure which can be seen in the centre foreground, to the left of the telephone box. The spire of St Giles Cathedral, next to which the infamous Tolbooth prison was situated, is visible in the background although it cannot actually be glimpsed from the Grassmarket. Beneath the apparent naturalism of Andrews's work lies a subtle reordering of the real world: this painting is a conflation of several views, recorded by him in photographs. He retained the drips which he thought of as redolent of the tears and the rain that are part of the history of the location.

Oil on canvas, 183 × 274.3
Purchased with assistance
from the National Art
Collections Fund 1993
GMA 3697

Francis Bacon 1909–92 · *Study for a Portrait 1991* 1991

Oil and pastel on canvas,
198 × 147.5
Accepted by H.M.
Government in lieu of
inheritance tax; presented
1995
GMA 3914

This painting, one of Bacon's last, is a portrait of the artist Anthony Zych (born 1958). Between August 1990 and September 1991 Bacon did three large paintings of Zych: this is the second, dating from March 1991. The first shows Zych leaning on a barrier at Chantilly racecourse, while the third, the artist's last painting, resembles a Crucifixion. Our work depicts Zych entering a room. Like many of Bacon's works, it too is based on photographs. Zych recalls: 'I think the painting shows me entering his studio [in South Kensington, London], or more likely his living quarters, reflected in the very large mirror there which occupied the better part of the wall facing the doorway onto the landing, although it could as easily be the doorway of one of the many restuaurants, bars and casinos we used to go to.' The table or tripod element in front of the figure is taken from a much earlier painting, *Three Studies for Figures at the Base of a Crucifixion* of 1944, in the Tate Gallery.

Leon Kossoff b.1926 · Between Kilburn and Willesden Green, Winter Evening 1992

Kossoff was born in London. Like Frank Auerbach (see p.180), he was taught by David Bomberg (see p.109). In common with Auerbach, Kossoff has concentrated on portraits of family and close friends and, in particular, on London landscapes.

Kossoff has been making paintings of railway landscapes in London since the early 1950s and he has also, in recent years, painted railway and underground stations. For several years in the early 1960s he had a studio adjacent to Willesden junction. *Between Kilburn and Willesden Green, Winter Evening* shows diesel and electric trains passing one another on railway lines running at the foot of the artist's garden in north London. It is a particularly fresh example of Kossoff's urban landscapes, in which racing clouds, swaying trees, hurtling and tilting railway carriages and a cold afternoon light, all combine to give an impression of rapid movement and change. Paradoxically, this image of transience is realised in almost glutinous paint, lending it a tangible and enduring physical presence.

Oil on board,
119.5 × 147.5
Purchased with assistance
from the National Art
Collections Fund 1994
GMA 3821

Sol LeWitt b.1928 · Five Modular Structures (Sequential Permutations on the Number Five) 1972

LeWitt is one of a number of mainly American artists active in the 1960s who were called Minimalists (others include Carl Andre, Robert Morris, Donald Judd and Dan Flavin). Compared to the work of the Abstract Expressionists, their work appeared machine-made and devoid of subjective expression. Minimalism does, however, have recognisable stylistic features, notably geometry and a concern with logical, modular structures. Emerging at the same time as Pop Art, Minimalist Art also responds (though in an entirely different way) to post-war consumerism.

Many of LeWitt's works deal with cubes. In this work, each of the five structures occupies the same ground plan. The structures rise in single steps to a height of five units; the fifth structure is uniformly five units tall. The permutations are simple, clear and logical, and the viewer is invited to follow the mental process and imagine other variations or orders. Although LeWitt's work appears objective, it is evident that any number of alternative permutations might be made. An apparently banal object can thus engage the viewer in very close attention and provoke imaginative responses. LeWitt has stated: 'The most interesting characteristic of the cube is that it is relatively uninteresting ... Therefore it is the best form to use as a basic unit for any more elaborate function, the grammatical device from which the work may proceed.' The emphasis on mental strategies makes him a forerunner of Conceptual Art.

Wood, enamel paint, each structure 62 × 98 × 62
Purchased 1974
GMA 1308

Dan Flavin 1933–96 · *Homage to V.Tatlin* 1975

Flavin began his career as a meteorologist and had almost no formal art training. However, like Judd (see p.188) he studied art history at Columbia University in the late 1950s. He began working with electric lights in 1961, producing works such as a flowerpot containing a lightbulb. He made his first fluorescent light works in 1963, fixing one to a wall at a 45 degree angle. From that time he worked exclusively with fluorescent lights, placing them on walls, tucking them discretely into corners, and sometimes standing them on the floor. As with much Minimalist Art, Flavin's work is intimately concerned with the space in which it is shown, and it therefore foreshadows 'installation' art. The choice of a banal, mass-produced, 'modern' object which nevertheless has a satisfying and arresting form, has close parallels with the iconography of contemporary Pop Art – Warhol's Brillo boxes, for example.

This is one of a series of works dedicated to the Russian Constructivist artist Vladimir Tatlin (1885–1953) who treated art almost in engineering terms. Flavin's first such work dates from 1965. Of that work, Flavin remarked: ' ... it memorialises Vladimir Tatlin, the great revolutionary, who dreamed of art as science.' He also stated that his work was 'founded in the young tradition of a plastic revolution which gripped Russian art only forty years ago.' Like Popova's paintings (see p.32) his works are clear, purposeful and non-illusionistic.

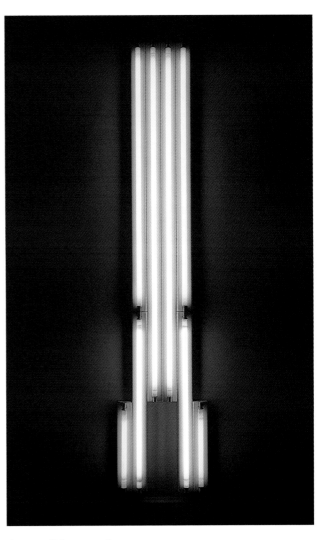

Fluorescent lights, 305 × 61 × 12
Purchased 1983
GMA 2799

Donald Judd 1928–94 · *Progression* 1978

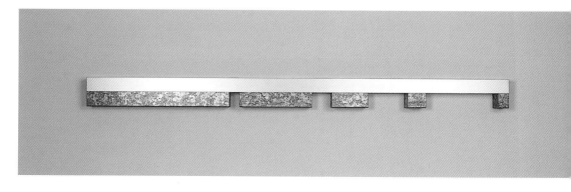

Chartreuse anodised aluminium and galvanised steel, 13 × 190.5 × 12.7
Purchased 1982
GMA 2504

Judd was a painter before he became a sculptor and he was also a noted art critic. In the early 1960s he made works which were part painting, part relief sculpture, and in 1963 he made his first fully three-dimensional pieces, initially from wood. Like LeWitt (see p.186), Judd based his work on simple mathematical formulae in order to avoid subjective, 'expressive' qualities. *Progression* employs the same form and dimensions as a work Judd had made in 1964 and which he repeated, using different colours and materials, in several sculptures of the 1970s. 'Reading' the work from right to left, the solid, galvanised steel blocks increase by fractionally under double size, while the spaces between them do the same, but in reverse. The smallest space and the smallest solid have the same dimensions. There is a deliberate intention to make art which looks as if it has not been made by hand but by machine (much of his work, including this piece, was fabricated by the firm of Bernstein Bros., on Long Island). Rejecting expression, description, symbol and metaphor, Judd aimed to reduce sculpture to its most basic constituents and make work that was exactly what it was, and nothing more. As with Flavin's work (see p.187), the form and the materials are intimately related: this tendency recalls the vogue for 'truth to materials', associated with early twentieth-century carving (see p.107). Like much Minimalist Art, *Progression* could even exist simply as a diagram with a series of instructions.

Anthony Caro b.1924 · *Table Piece* CCCLXXXVIII 1977

Having studied engineering and then art at the Royal Academy schools, from 1951 to 1953 Caro worked as an assistant to Henry Moore. In the 1950s he made figurative bronzes which were influenced by Moore. Caro met the American critic and champion of Abstract Expressionism,Clement Greenberg (see p.144), in 1959 and later in the year spent several months in the USA, where he met some of the leading young artists of the time, including David Smith, who made welded sculpture.

Immediately on his return to London Caro abandoned bronze for welded metal constructions composed of prefabricated girders and pipes. Compared to modelling and carving, the sculptor can create much more expansive, open forms with welded metal. Large, abstract, architectural compositions which stood directly on the floor, Caro's work of this period influenced a whole generation of sculptors.

Caro began to make small Table Piece sculptures in 1966, and since then has made several hundred (ours is number 388). While he makes his large, floor-placed sculptures in a vast studio, the Table Pieces are made at home in his garage. Owing to their manageable scale, they have the freedom of drawings, yet they are not models for larger works. Entirely abstract and composed of a remarkable vocabulary of forms – sprightly lines, arabesques, circles, pauses and full stops – they have parallels with dance and music.

Steel, rusted and varnished, 101.5 × 114.5 × 60
Purchased 1981
GMA 2464

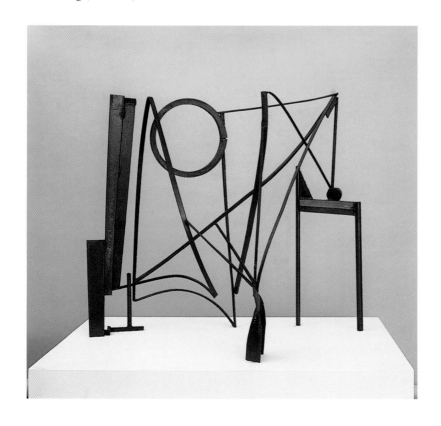

Broodthaers was born in Brussels. He had a varied early career, being amongst other things a book-dealer, poet, art critic, gallery guide and film maker. He was on the fringes of the Belgian Surrealist group and became friendly with Magritte (see pp.78–79). He was reluctant to have a conventional career and only began making art objects as a casual experiment when he was forty years old. His first work consisted of copies of his own unsold books of poems embedded into wet plaster, thereby making them unreadable. Subsequent works were concerned with food and its containers: mussel shells, eggs, chips and preservative jars, stuck together or altered so that they assumed a new identity. Broodthaers's interests parallel those of the Pop artists in the use of commonly available objects, but have a more intellectual flavour. His use of jam jars is more equivocal than, for example, Warhol's soup can: here he opens up a range of ideas about voyeurism and consumer culture. A literate, intellectual man, Broodthaers's outlook was similar to Duchamp's (see pp.66–67) in its ironic, self-questioning stance. Much of his later work was concerned with the practice and meaning of collecting and with the relationship between language, art and money. He opened his own Museum of Modern Art, initially installed in his Brussels flat, which included packing cases for pictures, postcards, reproductions, texts and other ephemera, but no 'art'.

Glass jars, wood and
magazine illustrations,
88.7 × 49.7 × 49.7
Purchased 1983
GMA 2794

A Luftwaffe pilot during the war, Beuys was shot down over the Crimea and was saved by peasants. Barely alive, he was wrapped in felt and fat, and taken to safety on sledges pulled by dogs. This incident, and these particular elements, informed much of his art, which has a redemptive, mystical and ritualistic character. Most of his work was in the form of 'Actions', involving teaching, audience discussion and performance. The recurrent themes were social and political: 'social sculpture', he called it. Beuys has something in common with Duchamp (see pp.66–67), though the aim is spiritual and shamanistic rather than ironic. His method of work has been immensely influential. Associated with the ecological movement, he also had a strong influence in German politics.

Beuys visited Edinburgh on three occasions in the early 1970s, each time at the invitation of gallery director Richard Demarco. This work was made in a dilapidated former poorhouse building in Edinburgh in June 1974. Beuys walked slowly around the edges of the room, offering up the old cooking pots to each of the walls. The pots had emotive links with the old poorhouse and represented, Beuys said, thinking, feeling and will. The pots were put on the floor and tied to a pair of blackboards on which Beuys made notes relating to his talk. *Three Pots for the Poorhouse* is therefore not so much an art work as a record or embodiment of this 'Action'.

Two blackboards with chalk, three cast iron pots, cord. Boards 117.5 × 119.5 and 120 × 119.2; pots 13 × 28.5 × 21 each
Purchased 1974
GMA 1318

Ian Hamilton Finlay b.1925

*Even Gods Have Dwelt
in Woods*
1976/83
Stone, 23 × 28.1 × 7.4
Scottish Arts Council
Collection: presented 1997
GMA 4180

Finlay was born in 1925 in the Bahamas. His family returned to Scotland when he was a child. He attended Glasgow School of Art for a brief period, served in the army and, in the 1950s, worked as a labourer and shepherd in the Orkney Isles. During the 1950s he wrote short stories and poems and in 1961 he co-established the Wild Hawthorn Press, which has published much of his printed work. In 1966 he moved to an isolated farmhouse in the Pentland Hills, south of Edinburgh, where he has made a remarkable garden called Little Sparta. He has developed an art which presents a challenging and often complex fusion of poetry, graphic art, sculpture and landscape gardening. The work is executed by assistants, following his instructions.

In the early 1960s Finlay began publishing 'concrete poetry', poems which rely on shape, structure and repetition of words rather than on syntax or narrative. Much of his work of the mid-1960s used fishing boats and the sea as a point of departure, playfully associating words with visual images. In the 1970s he turned his attention increasingly to themes of classicism, neo-classicism and warfare and in the 1980s to the subject of the French Revolution. Employing a broad range of texts ranging from classical philosophy and revolutionary slogans to art manifestos and newspaper headlines, Finlay investigates the power of images and symbols, particularly those associated with militarism, politics, art, classicism and nature. He frequently makes the analogy between war and the forces of Nature, highlighting the thin line that exists between creation and destruction, order and disorder, culture and chaos. *Even Gods Have Dwelt in Woods* and *The Medium is the Message* (one of many such prints) both refer to a long-running 'battle' with Strathclyde Regional Council over the rateable status of a Garden Temple on the artist's property. The carving, one of two made in 1976 and bought by the Scottish Arts Council, was subsequently 'kidnapped' by the artist's associates and inscribed on the reverse with the names of the 'war guilty'.

Never leaving his Little Sparta home, Finlay has developed an idiosyncratic and erudite body of work which has few parallels in twentieth-century art. The Gallery has a collection of more than 700 of Finlay's prints, cards and booklets and a number of sculptures, carved inscriptions and installations.

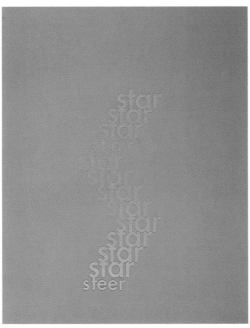

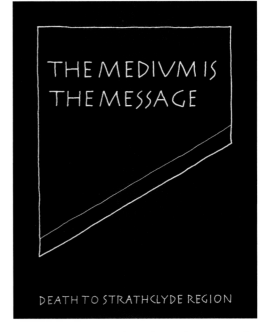

Coastal Boy (Fishing Boat: A534) 1977
Wood, painted, 26 × 244.5 × 6.5
Purchased 1992
GMA 3603

Star / Steer 1966
Screenprint on paper, 57 × 44.3
Purchased 1975
GMA A4.417

The Medium is the Message 1987
Screenprint on paper, 76 × 58.5
Purchased 1992
GMA A4.645

Duane Hanson 1925–96 · Tourists 1970

Hanson was born in Minnesota. He lived in Germany in the 1950s, then settled in Florida. He was one of a number of sculptors, including George Segal and John de Andrea, who took to casting figures from life in the 1960s. Hanson's first life casts, dating from 1967, had a political and social realist edge, referring to the Vietnam war and the race riots. In 1970 he began casting working-class figures in ordinary, mundane situations: a woman with her shopping trolley, a housewife reading, and these *Tourists*, perhaps Hanson's best-known work. Like the Pop artists, with whom he is often associated, Hanson was interested in the banality of consumer society.

The figures are cast from real people, then painted and dressed. The male and female figures seen here were cast one after the other in Hanson's studio and they never even met. His figures are generally caught in some private reverie, off guard and often bored. (Like Warhol, Hanson identified boredom and banality as key characteristics of postwar western society.) Most of them are fat, partly because, Hanson said, he found a bigger form more satisfactory in sculptural terms. Although they are funny, his works are also thought-provoking. They are exactly the type of people (overweight, unattractive, badly dressed, non-heroic) one would not expect to be made into sculptures. They exude a normality and humanity with which we can identify.

Polyester resin and fibreglass, painted in oil, and mixed media.
Man 152 high; woman 160 high
Purchased 1979
GMA 2132

John Davies b.1946 · For the Last Time 1970–72

Born in Cheshire, Davies studied sculpture at the Slade School of Art, London, under Reg Butler (see p.153). In the late 1960s he began making body and head casts in plaster, incorporating glass eyes and clothing the figures in real clothes. These disturbing works were first shown in Davies's solo exhibition at the Whitechapel Art Gallery in London in 1972. *For the Last Time*, shown in that exhibition, was his most complex work to date.

The figures can be placed in an infinite number of positions to suggest various meanings. Thus a certain formation can give the impression that the crawling figures are menacing the seated figure while another formation can suggest that the three masked figures are controlled by the seated figure and are threatening the viewer. The exact relationship between the characters is enigmatic, but they seem to have an unpleasant surprise in store for someone. Davies has written that he wanted the group to express feelings of repression and brutality, and the humiliating rituals employed by oppressors: 'I remember trying in my work to find a ring of truth about existence and behaviour, however unlikely the work might have to look as a result.'

Mixed media. Standing figure 181 high
Purchased 1989
GMA 3450

Boyle Family · *Addison Crescent Study (London Series)* 1969

*Painted fibreglass and
mixed media,*
247 × 244 × 19
Purchased 1974
GMA 1304

Mark Boyle was born in Glasgow in 1934. He became involved in theatre and Performance Art in the early 1960s. In 1964 he and his companion Joan Hills (born 1936) made their first replica of a section of ground. The works are made by spreading a plastic substance called Epikote on the ground. When removed it lifts up all the surface debris; it is then given a fibreglass support and is painted. This was the start of a project, 'The Journey to the Surface of the Earth', launched in 1968–69, the aim of which was to duplicate 1,000 randomly selected portions of the earth's surface. Darts were thrown blindfold at a map of the world to pinpoint proposed sites. The Boyles would travel to the site, throw a T-square in the air, and make an exact duplicate, normally 6 × 6 feet square, of the area where it landed. Another group of works, 'The London Series', focuses on west London: *Addison Crescent Study* is part of that series. Operating under the name Boyle Family, their two children have assisted with the production of these works. In 1966 Boyle observed: 'I have tried to cut out of my work any hint of originality, style, superimposed design, wit, elegance or significance. The aim is to produce as objective a work as possible'.

Bruce McLean b.1944 · *Landscape Painting* 1968

LANDSCAPE · PAINTING '68

*Colour photograph and transfer text, 31.2 × 31
Purchased 1990
GMA 3572*

Born in Glasgow, McLean studied at Glasgow School of Art and, from 1963 to 1966, at St Martin's School of Art in London where the leading so-called New Generation sculptors (King, Tucker, Bolus) were teaching. Influenced by Anthony Caro (see p.189), still an occasional tutor there, the students made formalist, floor-based sculpture in materials such as steel and fibreglass. McLean adopted this approach for a time but by 1967 was beginning to satirise such work, instead placing bits of junk in tasteful compositions on the pavement or road or in his sitting room. These works led to others in which mud and ice were arranged to form abstract sculpture.

Landscape Painting is one of a group of photographs which record 'sculptures' made at Largybeg on the Isle of Arran in 1968. They all feature a huge roll of photographic paper on which McLean spilt water-based paint to make, literally, landscape paintings. Deliberately undermining the self-importance of much contemporary art, these ephemeral works were thrown away after being photographed. They also make a witty comment on Land Art which was becoming popular in the late 1960s.

Hamish Fulton b.1946 *A Four Day Walk across the Border Country of England and Scotland, West Coast to East Coast from the Solway Firth to Holy Island, Early Spring 1977*, 1977

Three black and white photographs on card with transfer-text, 96 × 244
Purchased 1980
GMA 2201

Fulton was born in London to Scottish parents. He studied at St Martin's School of Art from 1966 to 1968, at the same time as Richard Long (see opposite), Bruce McLean (see p.197) and Gilbert and George (see p.201). Their work marked a move away from easel painting and three-dimensional sculpture towards conceptually-based work which negated traditional methods of composition and meaning. Influenced by the ecological movement, Fulton and Long in particular sought to make a new type of landscape art which used the landscape itself rather than being a painted or sculpted imitation of it.

Since 1969 Fulton's work has been specifically concerned with the experience of walking. From 1969 and throughout the 1970s his walks were represented in the form of black and white photographs made on the walks, with accompanying titles and texts. Many of the walks have been made in Scotland. Unlike Long with whom he has made a number of walks, Fulton does not alter the form of the landscape he walks in but photographs it or records it in words. Since the early 1980s he has increasingly used texts rather than photographs.

Richard Long b.1945 · *Stone Line 1980*

Long was born in Bristol, where he still lives. His work is about walking and the direct experience of nature. From the mid-1960s, while still a student, he began making walks and photographed the trace he had made (the flattened grass, stones laid at regular intervals) or would simply mark the course of the walk on a map. Through minimal intervention he expressed man's relationship with the landscape.

On walks made during the 1970s he began laying rocks or twigs in straight lines or circles. Lines and circles are ancient, primitive signs (recalling Stonehenge for example), and they have the same simplicity and grandeur as the landscape itself. By the late 1970s he was reconstructing these works in interior settings, though the walk remained the basis for collecting the natural material. He remarks: 'I do the things that have a deep meaning for me. I have the most profound feelings when I am walking or touching natural materials in natural places. That is what I've decided to do and that is what I am showing you in my art.' The slate for this work came from Delabole in Cornwall: it was Long's first work in slate.

Slate, 10 × 183 × 1067
Purchased 1980
GMA 2196

Barry Flanagan b.1941 · *Hello Cello* 1976

Clipsham stone, 40.6 x 25.5 x 22.9;
constructed wood base, 96 x 41 x 41
Bequeathed by Gabrielle Keiller 1995
GMA 3977

Flanagan was born in Prestatyn, North Wales. In the late 1960s he was one of a number of British sculptors who rejected the traditional materials of sculpture (stone, bronze, wood or even the steel girders favoured by the previous generation of British sculptors) for materials such as rope, sackcloth, branches or sand for use in installation projects. However, he took up carving in 1973, learning the techniques in a carving studio at Pietrasanta in Italy, which specialised in monumental carving and ornamental stonework. In the studio the head carver would rapidly engrave the block with a chisel, marking out the form which an assistant would then translate into three dimensions. Flanagan appropriated the method in his sculptures, engraving different forms on each of the sides of a stone block. It was the point at which the 'sculpture' subsumes the block that interested Flanagan, and whether he could set the two in balance. As he remarked: 'to what degree can the original character of the piece of stone be retained; to what degree must it be sacrificed in the pursuit and realisation of the carved image?'

In *Hello Cello* three of the sides depict parts of a figure from the shoulders down, while the fourth side depicts a cello. The sculpture, originally conceived as a freestanding object, was exhibited in that state in Flanagan's one-man show in the British Pavilion at the 1982 Venice Biennale. The wooden plinth element, which is riveted together, originated in Flanagan's designs for seating at the Hayward Gallery in London. It was made at a later date specifically for the sculpture.

Gilbert & George · *Exhausted* 1980

Italian-born Gilbert Proesch (b.1943) and Englishman George Passmore (b.1942) met and studied at St Martin's School of Art in London in 1967 and have made only collaborative works since then. In 1969 they performed the first of several 'living sculptures' which rapidly launched their international careers as leading British performance artists.

Besides performances Gilbert & George developed a variety of art forms suited to the portrayal of themselves as both artists and subjects of their art, including mural size drawings and paintings in which they depicted themselves self-consciously posing in landscape settings.

Throughout the 1970s, however, photography became their preferred medium and their output of large scale 'photo sculptures' like *Exhausted* (1980) has been immense. In the 1980s new subjects began to dominate their work, mostly derived from their immediate neighbourhood in the East End of London – visions of alienated youth, human despair and urban decay. Gilbert & George nevertheless continued to include themselves in some of the photo pieces and *Exhausted* is a self-portrait of the artists, Gilbert above and George below.

The child-like portrait drawings are wilfully clumsy, a feature that is exaggerated by their huge magnification and adds to their irony since they are clearly not the work of a child. Like many of the photo pieces of this period *Exhausted* has an air of menace. The photographs are printed on yellow-based paper which tends to distance the viewer and emphasises the artificial and contrived procedure with which the piece is made, each photograph being enlarged, printed and framed individually.

Sixteen-part photographic work (each part dyed and framed), 242 x 202 (assembled)
Purchased 1982
GMA 2507

Georg Baselitz b.1938

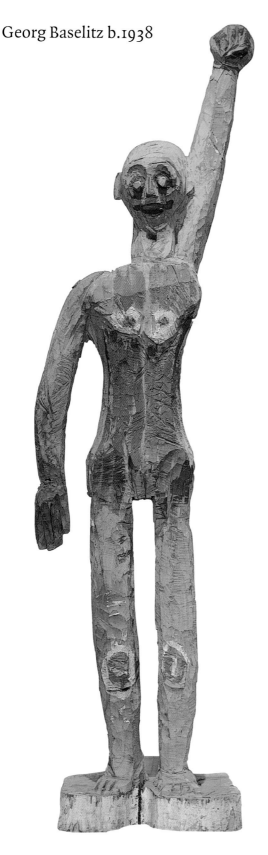

Georg Kern was born in Deutsch–baselitz, near Dresden in East Germany. He studied at art school in East Berlin in 1956, was expelled, and then from 1957 to 1962 studied in West Berlin. In 1961, the year the Berlin Wall was built, he adopted the name of his birthplace. During the late 1950s the dominant trend in East German art was socialist realism, while in West Germany abstraction reigned supreme. Baselitz's achievement in the early 1960s was to reintroduce the figure as well as a sense of history (a problematic issue in postwar Germany) into German painting, though he did this in a deeply sceptical and ambivalent way. In his series of 'Hero' paintings of 1965–66 he knowingly recycled the Romantic concept of the artist as lonely hero at odds with society. *Large Head*, one of Baselitz's earliest woodcut prints, dates from just after his scholarship stay in Florence, where he became particularly interested in Italian Mannerist painting. The fractured face, overlaid with worm-like forms, is characteristic of his contemporaneous paintings in which parts of the figures are cut up and rearranged or are missing. He deliber-ately countered conventions, sometimes painting with his fingers instead of

opposite page

Untitled (Ohne Titel)
1982–84
Limewood and oil paint,
253 × 71 × 46
Purchased with assistance
from the National Art
Collections Fund (William
Leng Bequest) 1989
GMA 3530

Large Head
(Grosser Kopf) 1966
Colour woodcut and
monotype on paper,
50.1 × 40.9
Purchased 1988
GMA 3374

Pillow (Kopfkissen)
1987
Oil on canvas, 200 × 162.2
Purchased 1988
GMA 3372

brushes and, after 1969, almost always painted the motif upside-down. In doing so, he was exploring the area between the two dominant trends in modern art, abstraction and figuration.

Baselitz began making sculpture in 1979, carving a huge tree trunk with chainsaws and axes. Trees feature in many of his paintings and the fact that he originally planned to work in forestry may relate to his preference for wood. He has remarked that 'In sculpture, using the saw is an aggressive process which is the equivalent of drawing … By working in wood, I want to avoid all manual dexterity, all artistic elegance, everything to do with construction.' His sculpture has obvious associations with African art, but also lies within the long tradition of German wood carving, which, in the early twentieth century, was revived by Expressionist painters such as Kirchner (see pp.44–45). This untitled work is one of his largest and earliest carvings. Far from being a Nazi salute, as has been suggested, the raised arm derives from African carvings of figures who raise their arms to signal surrender in battle. A drawing of the same figure has him holding a flag.

Sandro Chia b.1946 · *Courageous Boys at Work* 1981

Chia was born in Florence. He is one of a number of Italian figurative artists who came to prominence in the late 1970s and early 1980s and became known collectively as the *transavanguardia*; Francesco Clemente, Enzo Cucchi and Mimmo Paladino were others. Referring to the masters of the Italian Renaissance, they painted large, heroic figures who seemed to belong to some new, late twentieth-century mythology. Rejecting the cool intellectualism and political engagement of much art of the 1970s, large-scale figurative painting (often referred to as New Image Painting or Neo-Expressionism) became widespread throughout Europe and the USA in the early 1980s. Chia was one of the leading figures in this movement.

Chia's giant figures are almost always young men and are arguably alter egos of the artist; they are generally involved in a journey, though the object of their quest is unclear. The subject of *Courageous Boys at Work* is effectively autobiographical, for here the heroic figures are painters. Commenting on the work, Chia wrote (with tongue in cheek): 'I would like to say that those two courageous boys are painters at work because courageous boys are either firemen or painters.'

Oil and oil pastel on canvas, 168.2 × 158
Purchased 1982
GMA 2503

Mimmo Paladino b.1948 · Silent Blood (Silenzioso Sangue) 1979/85

Oil, wax and wood on canvas, 213.5 × 140
Purchased 1987
GMA 3017

Paladino was born in the south of Italy, near Benevento, and grew up in Naples. He lives in Benevento and Milan. Like Chia (see opposite), Paladino was one of a small group of Italian artists who rose to international prominence in the early 1980s. Their work offered a contemporary reinterpretation of classical mythology, and Paladino's work in particular is grounded in Etruscan art and in the classical art of his native area. His paintings seem to concern mysterious religious and pagan rituals and the world of the dead, but they escape specific interpretations. As Paladino remarks: ' ... the figures in my paintings, the animals, the masks, the theme of death – I do not want to explain or analyse them. They are the roots out of which the picture develops, but not its content.' He began making sculpture in 1982 and from that date incorporated sculptural elements into his canvases. Paladino painted *Silent Blood* in 1979 and reworked it several years later, adding the wooden head.

Steven Campbell b.1953 · *Elegant Gestures of the Drowned after Max Ernst* 1986

Campbell was born in Glasgow where he spent several years working in a steelworks. In 1978 he enrolled at Glasgow School of Art. He was initially involved in Performance Art and only began painting in about 1981. He lived in New York from 1982 to 1986 before returning to Scotland.

Campbell's paintings are characterised by surreal and deliberately confusing narratives. In his works, a tweed-clad, mainly male cast of characters roam the countryside, becoming embroiled in bizarre, apparently nonsensical activities. The stories of P.G. Wodehouse, murder mystery magazines and children's book illustrations have provided the inspiration for many of these works. They lie within a long British tradition of eccentric art (Hogarth, Stanley Spencer) yet do so with a certain irony. Campbell paints quickly, improvising as he works: 'If I know what I'm going to paint beforehand there's no point in painting it.'

In *Elegant Gestures of the Drowned after Max Ernst*, a suited figure (perhaps the artist's alter ego) wedges himself between St Christopher and the infant Christ, and seems intent on guiding the latter to a watery end. The sheep, the hilly landscape and the presence of the Union Jack may refer to the Falklands War of 1982.

Oil on canvas, 262 × 238.4
Purchased 1987
GMA 3296

Adrian Wiszniewski b.1958 · *Kingfisher* 1987

Acrylic and felt-tip pen on
canvas, 213.5 × 213.5
Purchased 1987
GMA 3042

Wiszniewski was born in Glasgow. He
studied architecture at the Mackintosh
School of Architecture, then studied at
Glasgow School of Art from 1979 to
1983. His first paintings date from
1983. His work lies within the poetic,
British romantic tradition of artists
such as Blake and Cecil Collins, but is
also informed by Surrealism.

Kingfisher was painted in 1987, two
days after the birth of the artist's son,
Max. It was preceded by a more
forbidding painting, *Gift Box*, which
features a raven-like bird delivering an
egg – emblematic of the worry prior to
the birth and parenthood. The bright
colours and arcadian theme in
Kingfisher reflect the artist's sense of
relief. The figures may be seen as the
artist and his son, while the kingfisher
doubles as the stork from fairytales,

delivering the baby. The fish also has a
child, which it spits out from its
mouth as the kingfisher grabs it.
Following his usual practice,
Wiszniewski drew directly onto the
canvas, without making preliminary
sketches, and then used a broad felt-
tip pen and acrylic paint. The spare use
of colour is unusual in his work.

Ken Currie b.1960 · *Template of the Future* (from *Glasgow Triptych*) 1986

Oil on canvas, 214 × 272.3
Purchased 1987
GMA 3012A

Like Campbell, Howson and Wisz-niewski, Currie studied at Glasgow School of Art. All four were taught by Alexander Moffat. After leaving the school Currie worked as a film-maker, but in 1985 he returned to painting.

This work is the first panel from the *Glasgow Triptych*. The triptych was, Currie stated, 'my first attempt in oil paint to sum up the … story of the Scottish working class in the 20th century, as reflected in the relationship between an old shop steward and political activist and a young unemployed man.' Of *Template of the Future*, which is the left-hand panel, Currie said that it 'recalls the moment of the Labour victory in 1945, as remembered by the old activist and retold to the young man in the City Bar'. The central panel, *The Apprentice*, treats the early

1980s as years of decay, while the third, *Young Glasgow Communists*, shows a group of young activists planning for the future. The triptych is inspired by the work of Léger (see especially p.137), the Mexican mural artists and the German *Neue Sachlichkeit* art of Grosz and Dix (see pp.57 and 62). Following completion of the *Glasgow Triptych* Currie painted a series of eight large paintings on the theme of Scottish labour history for The People's Palace museum in Glasgow.

Peter Howson b.1958 · *Just Another Bloody Saturday* 1987

Born in London, Howson moved to Glasgow at the age of four. He studied at Glasgow School of Art from 1975 to 1977, was briefly in the army, then returned to the art school from 1979 to 1981. He was a contemporary of Campbell, Wiszniewski and Currie, with whom he is often associated.

His paintings are mainly of the Glasgow underclass: dossers, drunks, body-builders and boxers (during his time in the army Howson was a keen boxer). At times Howson portrays this overtly working-class, masculine world, with sympathy and tenderness; at other times he portrays it as a seething hotbed of violence. While not portraying a specific match, *Just Another Bloody Saturday* recalls the famous rivalry between Glasgow Rangers and Celtic, the battle on the pitch mirroring the territorial struggle taking place in the terraces.

Oil on canvas, 211 × 274.7
Purchased 1987
GMA 3041

Bill Woodrow b.1948 · *Clamp* 1986

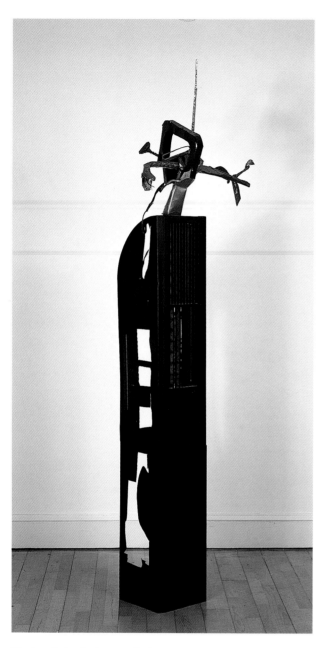

Woodrow studied at St Martin's School of Art, London, from 1968 to 1971. He was one of a number of sculptors born in the late 1940s who, in the early 1980s, spearheaded what became known as the New British Sculpture (others included Tony Cragg, Richard Deacon, Antony Gormley, Alison Wilding and Richard Wentworth). Their early work was mainly 'object based' in that rather than being carved or modelled, it began with a manufactured object.

Woodrow used discarded consumer products in his work of the 1970s but only in 1980 did he begin to make works in which junk objects – particularly domestic appliances – give birth to new, ingeniously cut and crafted 'surrogate' objects. A car door transforms itself into a cactus plant; a washing-machine plays host to a guitar; a bucket sprouts a lobster. Using metal shears and pliers, Woodrow created an absurd and magical world in which apparently unrelated objects were united. In *Clamp*, a section of ventilation ducting is transformed into a curious assortment of a snake-cum-branch, which is grasped by a golden fist and a transistor radio; this in turn is held together by a G-clamp. Although in Woodrow's work there is often no logical connection between the parent body and its 'offspring', this is, in part, a comment on the way in which late twentieth-century culture has reduced all subject matter to the same level and meaning.

Metal ventilation ducting, enamel paint,
248.5 × 67 × 51
Purchased 1986
GMA 3007

Alison Wilding b.1948 · Hand to Mouth 1986

Wilding was born in Blackburn. She studied at Ravensbourne College of Art and, from 1970 to 1973, at the Royal College of Art in London. *Hand to Mouth* is one of a number of works by Wilding featuring two connected yet dissimilar parts. A tall, three-sided leaded steel element towers above an egg-like form carved in wood and containing a small pool of beeswax. The carved form is rounded, warm and sensual – like an animal or a snail; the constructed steel structure is cold, smooth and evidently man-made, with the bolts clearly visible. The sliced apertures show that the steel part is hollow and thin-skinned while the carved part is a closed form with evident mass and density.

Although there are similarities with the work of Minimalist artists such as Donald Judd (see p.188), Wilding's work – like much of the so-called New British Sculpture – contains references to the human figure. The steel element is anthropomorphic in shape and scale, and the dialogue between the two elements is as much human as geometric. It seems that the smaller form is obstructing the path of the larger one; there may also be a suggestion of the relationship between mother and child. The title refers to two objects – the hand and mouth – which are part of the same context yet are located in different places and have different functions.

Leaded steel, brass, wood, lead and beeswax,
200 × 54 × 55; 29 × 47.5 × 32
Presented by the Contemporary Art Society
(Henry Moore Foundation Grant) 1992
GMA 3661

Gormley was born into a Catholic family and studied at a Benedictine school. He spent three years in India, where he took a keen interest in Buddhism. These biographical details are relevant in view of the strong spiritual quality which informs his work. On his return from India he studied sculpture at Goldsmiths' College of Art and at the Slade School of Art in London. His first lead body cases date from 1981. To make these the artist is wrapped in thin cloth and is coated in plaster; the plaster 'casing' is removed, strengthened with fibreglass, and is covered in roofing lead, which, after being beaten into place, is often soldered along the horizontal and vertical axes.

Present Time is based on two moulds made from the artist's body. The solid form of the lower figure and the horizontal divisions in the lead casing emphasise its weight, while its closed form evokes feelings of imprison-ment, isolation and withdrawal. The upper half, in contrast, with legs apart and outstretched, is free and expan-sive. *Heaven and Earth* and *Earth and Sky* were first considered as titles. Gormley comments that the work concerns 'the coming of the spirit into substance, the soul into the body, the mind into matter ... ' It concerns, then, our spiritual or mental states and our physical state: in *Present Time* these states are connected yet divided.

Lead, fibreglass, plaster and air,
340 × 193 × 35.5
Purchased with assistance from the Henry Moore Foundation 1990
GMA 3561

Callum Innes b.1962 · *Six Identified Forms* 1992

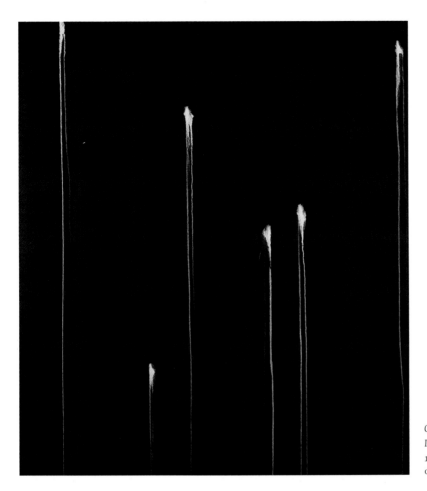

Oil on canvas, 220 × 190
Purchased (Knapping Fund)
1993
GMA 3670

Innes was born in Edinburgh. He studied at Gray's School of Art, Aberdeen, and at Edinburgh College of Art. He lives and works in Edinburgh. In the late 1980s, following an artist's residency in Amsterdam, he began to reduce the figurative content in his work. His first major series is the *Identified Forms* paintings, begun in 1990 and initially made on oiled paper, and subsequently made as large canvases. Rather than being built up through an accumulation of brush-strokes which eventually fill the canvas, Innes's paintings are made through a process of removal. For the *Identified Forms* paintings, the primed canvas was covered with a deep, olive-green or brown oil paint, brushed on in broad horizontal sweeps, and then dissolved with turpentine. Rather than being randomly formed, each of the rivulets is carefully created with a fine brush to expose the bare canvas beneath (this approach is the very opposite of drip painting or action painting). Hovering in the dark, the ambiguous stains suggest something natural and elemental, a state between solid and void, a wound. Innes remarks that 'My starting point is the desire to create an image that is somehow natural, that exists in its own right, holds a place for itself.'

Helen Chadwick 1953–96 · *Self-Portrait* 1991

Chadwick was born in London. Working with photography, she used her own body as the subject of her work, incorporating photographs of herself in large installations. In the late 1980s she took self-portraiture a step further, making exquisite Polaroid photographs of raw meat and innards: sexually provocative, they were suggestive of human flesh. Following these *Meat Abstracts* was a series of colour photographs sandwiched between glass plates and lit by electric lights. *Self-Portrait* belongs to this *Meat Lamps* series.

Self-Portrait shows the artist's own hands, gently cradling a disembodied, walnut-like brain. In the same way that, regardless of gender, age or race, everybody's flesh looks the same, so this is true of the brain. It is a portrait of all brains, a kind of collective self-portrait. When we look at the work our brain is effectively looking at itself (a potentially unsettling experience given that the brain is at the core of our identity). Commenting on another version of this work, Chadwick said: 'The oval locket of a cranium is opened to reveal an amatory vanitas more vital than the traditional melancholic emblem of mortality, the skull.'

Transparency, glass, aluminium and electrics,
50.9 × 44.6 × 11.8
Purchased by the Contemporary Art Society
with assistance from the Henry Moore
Foundation, and presented 1996
GMA 4096

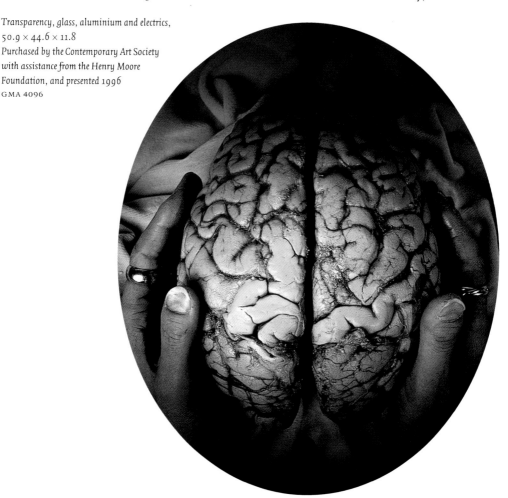

Rachel Whiteread b.1963 · *Demolished 1996*

Whiteread was born in London. In 1988 she began making casts of the insides of ordinary domestic objects, initially using wardrobes, and subsequently beds, floors, baths and even whole rooms. Cast in plaster, rubber or resin, the works duplicated the space within the objects in an arresting and richly metaphorical way. While having clear formal references to Minimalist sculpture, her negative casts also evoke the history of the objects – the people who used them and the things they once contained. In 1993 Whiteread made a cement cast of the inside of a terraced three-storey house in the London borough of Hackney, where she lives and works. Standing alone and making visible the private, anonymous space that countless unknown people had lived within, it stood as a poignant symbol of memory and mortality. *House* itself was demolished, amidst great controversy, in 1994.

Demolished, Whiteread's first print series, continues the theme explored in *House*. The prints originate in a set of twelve of the artist's own photographs, taken between October 1993 and June 1995, of buildings being demolished in Hackney. There are four images of three demolition sites (only one of the three sets is illustrated here). In the same way that Whiteread's negative casts suggest the trace of a human presence, so the tower blocks, with their connotations of social neglect and poverty, are evocative of the countless lives lived within them.

Portfolio of twelve screenprints,
each 48.9 × 74.4
Purchased 1997
GMA 4201

Stephan Balkenhol b.1957 · *Small Head Relief: Woman*
(Kleines Kopfrelief: Frau) 1995

Poplar wood, painted,
28.5 × 32 × 3.1
Purchased 1998
GMA 4216

Balkenhol was born in Fritzlar, West Germany. His work lies in the long tradition of woodcarving in Germany – from the Gothic period to the Expressionist sculpture of artists such as Kirchner and Barlach (see pp.44–45 and 61), and, more recently, Georg Baselitz (see pp.202–203). However, Balkenhol's figures represent the polar opposite of Expressionist angst. Abnormally normal, non-heroic types, they seem disengaged to the point of indifference or boredom. By leaving the process of making apparent in the rough-hewn marks of the chisel and in the summary colouring of the wood, Balkenhol emphasises that his works are sculptures as much as representations. Fashioned with admirable skill and simplicity, they are pieces of wood masquerading as people.

It has been pointed out that his neutral, post-heroic figures contrast with the giant, rhetorical statues beloved by totalitarian regimes, and that his work therefore comments on the fall of the Berlin Wall and the break-up of the Eastern Bloc countries. This may be true in part, but Balkenhol actually started working in this style in the early 1980s.

Kerry Stewart b.1965 · 'The Only Solution was to ...' 1997

Stewart was born in Paisley, near Glasgow. She studied German and the History of Art at Edinburgh University before attending Chelsea School of Art from 1989 to 1993. Stewart's subject matter is at once normal and bizarre: a nun lying on the ground, a pregnant schoolgirl, twin boys in identical clothes, a shifty-looking 'Manager' standing stiffly and solemnly in his three-quarter-length coat. Made as life-size plaster figures, her earlier works have the simplified forms and abrupt colouring associated with model toys or charity collection boxes. Po-faced and slightly sinister, they occupy a twilight zone between the real and the manufactured.

'The Only Solution was to ...' presents a small baby in a baby carrier. The baby is asleep in the shiny, leatherette-look chair, strapped in by a safety harness. The work is surprising and disconcerting, ordinary yet ambiguous. Stumbling across it on the floor, the viewer is at first inclined to accept it for the real thing and to look about for the absent parent. On closer inspection it turns out to be a facsimile. The subject itself is commonplace yet unlikely material for an artist. It is precisely this absence of dramatic or aesthetic potential that makes the work weird and compelling. The title invites the viewer to ponder upon what 'the only solution' might have been.

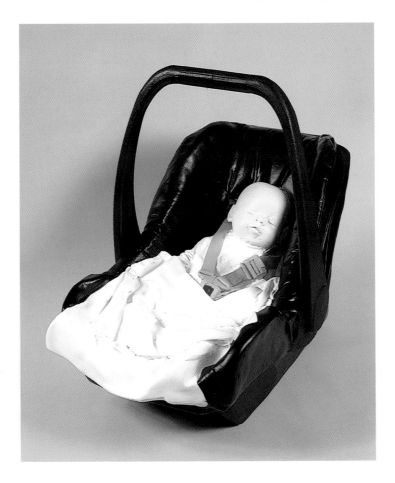

Plaster polymer and acrylic paint, 55.5 × 70 × 39
Purchased 1998
GMA 4210

Damien Hirst b.1965 · *Love Will Tear us Apart* 1995

Hirst was born in Bristol and grew up in Leeds, where he studied at the College of Art. From 1986 to 1989 he attended Goldsmiths' College of Art, London. *Love Will Tear us Apart* is one of a series, begun in 1989, of medicine cabinets containing bottles and packets of drugs. In common with Warhol and Bacon, the abiding theme in Hirst's work is death. Some of his works feature dead animals preserved in fluids while others feature surgical equipment and even cigarette butts. His coloured 'Spot Paintings' are all titled after chemicals. The medicine cabinets, in which the pharmaceutical products are neatly arranged on shelves, refer to our obsession with drugs, which have effectively replaced God in modern mythology. Drugs seem to hold the key to life and death: they have the power to kill and cure; they are also lifestyle accessories. Hirst remarks that the series is about 'the confidence that drugs will cure everything'. The syringes in this small cabinet are simultaneously attractive and threatening, pastel coloured and packed like sweets in a handy dispenser, yet potentially lethal. (As a child Hirst ate a packet of pills, thinking they were sweets, and had to have his stomach pumped.) A number of Hirst's works are titled after pop records. The title of this work is taken from a recording by Joy Division. The band's lead singer, Ian Curtis (1955–80), was noted for his dark, introspective lyrics, and following his suicide became something of an icon for those of Hirst's generation. This syringe cabinet was produced in an edition of thirty examples.

Plastic cabinet, needles and syringes,
35.5 × 50.9 × 22.3
Purchased 1998
GMA 4205

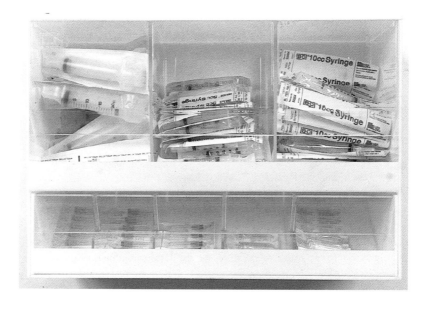

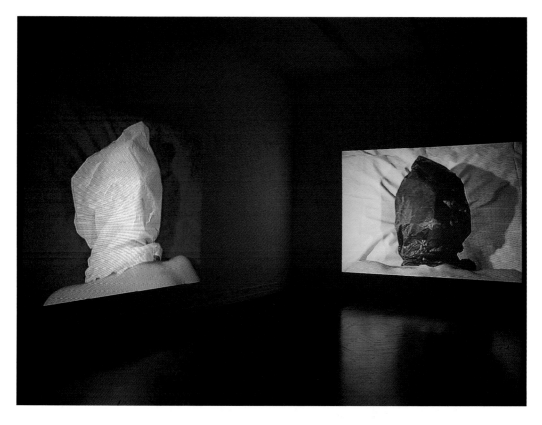

Stephanie Smith was born in Manchester in 1968 and studied at the Slade School of Art in London. Edward Stewart was born in Belfast in 1961 and studied at Glasgow School of Art. They met in 1991 when they were participating artists at the Rijksakademie van Beeldende Kunsten in Amsterdam, and since 1992 have worked in collaboration, mainly using video. They live in Glasgow.

Breathing Space comprises two wall-sized video projections, shown at right angles to each other. The videos are on a sixty-minute tape loop which plays continuously. The projections show two figures from the shoulders up, their heads covered by plastic bags. We hear the amplified sound of their constricted breathing, as the plastic is sucked in and expelled, rustling noisily. The two figures are separated yet united in their struggle. The bizarre scene carries associations of torture, violence and sado-masochism, but it is also visually arresting and full of black humour. Watching the motionless heads in a dark, claustrophobic space, we wonder whether this is some sort of game or punishment – or both. Their complicity in an action which every child is warned against implies an element of pleasure in danger but also danger in life, since breathing is a necessity. Smith and Stewart's work deals especially with the notion that pain and pleasure are interdependent parts of any relationship – that they perhaps define a relationship. Deliberately fraught with contradictions, this seemingly vicious work is about breath – the stuff of life.

Double colour video projection installation, with sound (dimensions variable)
Purchased 1998
GMA 4195

James Rielly b.1956 · *Hold* 1997

Rielly was born in Wales and lives in London. Dealing in particular with the theme of childhood and experience, Rielly's subjects include children with adult heads, identical twins, smiling children with slight deformities, pain and illness. The paintings are a mixture of the funny, the sinister and, often, the sexually provocative.

Like most of Rielly's paintings, *Hold* is a composite image derived from several different photographs. Artificially lit and stiffly composed, it bears all the hallmarks of a school portrait photograph, only there is an ambiguous red mark on the child's forehead. A wound, scar, growth or hole, it is emblematic of something wrong yet seems almost proudly displayed. The palid colour of the skin may suggest disease or illness, or even a faded photograph of a dead person. The title refers to the desire to 'hold' on to the present and fix it in the memory. Rielly presents a private world of pain and comedy and it is unclear whether the images are ironic, straightforward, deeply sad or deliberately provocative. The confused, fractured narrative is at the heart of their meaning.

Oil on canvas,
213.4 × 182.8
Purchased 1998

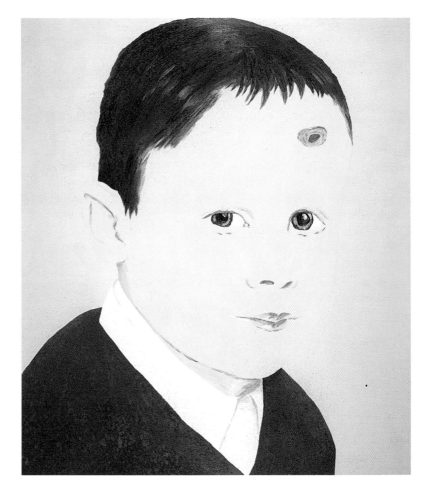

Richard Billingham b.1970 · *Untitled* 1995

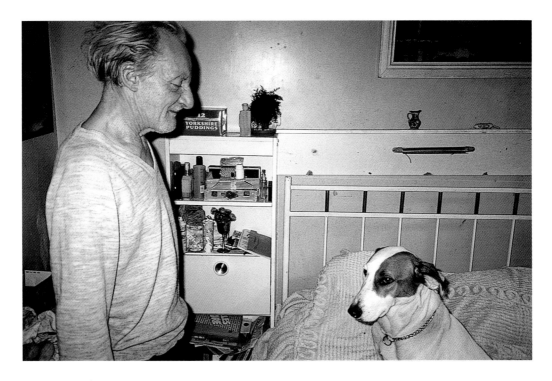

Billingham's large-scale photographs document the world of his father Raymond and his mother Elizabeth, at home in their flat on a housing estate in the West Midlands. Commenting on his domestic situation, Billingham states: 'My father is a chronic alcoholic. He doesn't like going outside and mostly drinks home-brew. My mother Elizabeth hardly drinks but she does smoke a lot. She likes pets and things that are decorative. They married in 1970 and I was born soon after.'

Billingham began taking snapshots of his family in about 1990, initially using them as study aids for his paintings, but subsequently seeing them as ends in themselves. The photographs are funny, but are also painful, poignant and slightly alarming. We see Ray and Liz, and sometimes their youngest son, Jason, sitting about at home, watching television, eating, drinking, arguing and doing nothing. It is a real-life 'kitchen-sink' family drama. The unposed photographs are often blurred and harshly lit, mirroring the *vérité* nature of the subject matter. The various pets play walk-on parts, but appear to represent the normative values in a dysfunctional and potentially hostile environment.

Colour photograph on aluminium, 80 × 120 Purchased 1998

Index of Artists

Copyright Acknowledgements